What some readers said...

The real strength of the United States of America has never been defined by land mass, population size or battles won. Indeed, we rank way down the list in many of these and other categories. What we excel in is our acceptance of change and difference.

In his recent work, Dr. Reza Mansoor describes the role of his Muslim brethren in the building of our nation. One has only to understand the precedent setting role of Muslims in medicine over the centuries to give credence to his assessment as to what is going on in his (our) country. Those who revere Islam have as much to do with America's success as do Protestants, Catholics, Jews, Hindus, or any other religious sect.

Sameness did not build America. Difference did. The misdeeds of a few at any given moment cannot blur the fact that we are a country of diverse ethnicity, different religions, different values, etc. What makes us brothers is our love of America.

This is what Dr. Mansoor's book celebrates.

Governor Lowell P. Weicker
Former Governor,
State of Connecticut

This is a compelling and down to earth description of the experience of being a normal American citizen who is Muslim, seeking to practice his faith in post 9/11 USA, in which overt acts of hatred and the willful mis-understanding of Islam on the part of some, have been mixed with acts of friendship and solidarity on the part of others. Dr Mansoor's response to his experience within the Muslim community has been one that seeks in multiple ways to strengthen its identity and its institutions within the USA. His response within the larger American society has been proactive engagement, seeking opportunities to portray Islam in an accurate light and reaching out and working with Jewish and Christian leaders, police departments, political representatives and many more. This is an account that will help those who are not Muslim understand and feel the experience and perspective of Muslims in America, and will help Muslims looking for constructive, positive action, by providing ideas and examples of just such action.

Dr Mansoor tells the reader "It begins with you, the reader taking the first step. You have to decide firstly not to be a foot soldier of hate... It means overcoming fear with education... Remember, learn about the other from the other, not those who fear or hate them." For those who would like to take the first step and learn, this is surely a great place to begin.

Dr. Heidi Hadsell
President,
Hartford Seminary

After the tragedy of 9/11, the body of our nation was bleeding and broken, providing an unfortunate environment for the disease of Islamophobia, this being but the latest form of xenophobia from which our country has suffered. During this time, Dr. Reza Mansoor, being the thoughtful and compassionate doctor that he is, provided extraordinary leadership in our interfaith community, holding in his gentle hands the broken body of our not-so-civil Civil Body Politic, until it had knit itself back together. Throughout this troubled decade, Dr. Mansoor has helped us to see the true face of Islam, a face badly distorted by the fear mongers in our society. In his own example, he has helped us to see that Islam is a religion of peace and tolerance, courage and resilience. Drawing on the deep roots of Islam, Dr. Mansoor helped us all to go deeper into our own faith traditions so we could find that sacred common ground so necessary for peace and reconciliation. In this book, we have the great privilege of witnessing the personal journey of Dr. Mansoor, his love for our country and his personal perspective on the vital work of our interfaith community. This book is an important book for all those who yearn to see the true face of Islam, but also, it's a book that will inspire us to open the doors of our own faith communities to work together with others to make this world a better and more peaceful place for our children.

Rev. David W. Good
Minister Emeritus
The First Congregational Church of Old Lyme

It is a cri de coeur but in a tone that is far from any shrieking or shouting. This is a book written by a man, who has his daily calling to attend to the needs of patients suffering from various heart diseases. Maybe this reality plays into how Reza Mansoor deals with a watershed moment of our time for Muslims throughout the world. It is written in a very personal style. You feel like you are sitting very close to Reza as he is sharing his experiences of what it means to be a Muslim in the US today. It is a cri de coeur, because it is heartrending to read how Islam and Muslims today in many parts of the Western world are being looked upon with suspicion and distrust, the victims of defamation, often driven by hate. "Too many American Muslims are still scared to be known as Muslims due to the negative stereotypes of Muslims and that is a sad but true fact." Reza rightly asks how the cherished principle of freedom of speech is taken as "an excuse to insult". How can it be in order for media "to spearhead hatred of any group" in society? It is frightening to read how media personalities, politicians, lobby-groups and Christian and Jewish leaders under the guise of "patriotism" use their platforms to advocate discrimination of Muslims in the US and to realize how this has fed into increasingly intrusive laws and law enforcement, singling out the Muslim community.

It is something worth reflecting on and to take to heart, when Reza writes about those who once left dictatorial regimes and oppression for the dream of the freedom of the USA and now increasingly see how the US through its legislation, the PATRIOT Act, the National Defense Authorization Act is becoming more and more like the states the immigrants and refugees once fled from.

But this book is not only a cri de coeur; it is also a call to Muslims in the US to refuse being defined by the other, to challenge among

Muslims themselves any perception that "accepts" being a victimised community. Reza's book is a call to Muslims to contribute creatively to open houses for new exchanges, new alliances and networks with people of different faiths, prepared to work together for a plural society, where respect for the other is a common value.

Rev. Dr. Hans Ucko,
Former Program Secretary for Interreligious Relations and Dialogue
World Council of Churches,
Geneva.

After the terrorist attacks of 9/11, American Muslims faced an environment of extraordinary pressure and tension. While sharing the anxieties of other Americans living under the threat of more attacks, Muslims were also horrified and traumatized by how their faith was hijacked by militant extremists. Then things got worse. Political and religious bigots generated a climate of hatred towards Muslims and were even successful creating discriminatory legislation and regulations against them. Into this climate of fear and bigotry stepped many heroes: ordinary Muslims who reclaimed the voice of Islam and their interfaith partners who stood beside them for the common good. In his memoir, Reza Mansoor tells the compelling story of his community and how they faced these challenges together.

Dr. Ingrid Mattson,
Past President,
Islamic Society of North America

First, let me say, Reza, what an honor and privilege it was to be given the manuscript of your book to read. And a most interesting read it was. I have always found you a passionate and faithful member of your community but to have had the privilege of "accompanying" you on your personal journey was deeply moving. You are obviously a man of great feeling and enormous belief.

All of this helps to explain the ground out of which your views of history grow and the sensitivity with which you explain what it is to be a Muslim-American today. It is ever increasingly more important for all Americans to see your perspective and to understand one another.

While the lens through which we understand the Middle East and its tragic modern politics are not always the same, we must always be open to each other's narrative. It will only be the mutual hope and confidence that arises out of the commonalities of our faith traditions---the idea that justice and peace are not ours to impose, but are Divine gifts and imperatives---that will help us overcome human antipathy toward the "other," someone different.

Your manuscript is crowned with a faithful confidence that Justice and Peace are possible which will make it a requirement to be read by open-minded people who wish to share your confidence. Your integrity and decency can be found in the spaces between the words.

Reza, this is not easy work but your dedication frankly inspires many of us who may not share all of your ideology, nevertheless are compelled to engage with you, to learn from you, and to reach across any false barriers without fear. And it is personally an honor to do so.

Rabbi Herbert Brockman, PhD
Congregation Mishkan Israel
Lecturer, Yale Divinity School
New Haven, CT

Dr. Reza's awe-inspiring book is a must read for the wide awake person who wants to know the truth about the so-called "Muslim-Threat." It is full of heart wrenching points that cannot be argued with. This is a story that needed to be told, not by a celebrated

Imam or great Islamic scholar, but by a professional person, a medical doctor with hands on experience. A concerned person who decided to not just sit around and watch what is going on, but someone who decided to fight back in the best manner.

Dr Reza lays out a clear blue print for Muslims to be successful in overcoming the Islamophopia that permeates our society. He shows the reader how to build bridges of understanding of the other. He demonstrates clearly the road to take to begin to respect and appreciate others, for anyone who is interested in breaking the ugly cycle of intolerance.

Anyone who takes the time to read this book has to come away with a deeper appreciation of their Muslim neighbors, recognizing that Muslims are not the enemy. The enemy is the hate mongers who are desperately trying to give Islam a black eye.

Dr. Reza names the leading protagonist and their supporters. He gives evidence after evidence of their mistaken notions, as well as the lies that they have put all over the social network.

What I really like about this book is Dr. Reza doesn't just identify the problems that exist, he gives examples of successful strategies that can be used to eliminate those problems. He gives the reader countless stories about the great work that continues to be done in Connecticut by those Muslims who have made it their business to be pro-active! Muslims, who have been called to action to improve the image of the Muslims, not by talking or being seen in nicely placed photo ops, but by getting involved with issues that effect and concern the communities.

In describing some of the work that has been done Dr. Reza has textual support from the Qur'an. Muslims ought to be about getting to know their neighbors. He has done just that, realizing that you never get to truly know a person until and unless you work with them. Dr. Reza tells his story about how he came to America, the land of freedom and opportunity, and how like other immigrants he has grown to love and appreciate this great land. He speaks about

the events of 9/11 and the spiral downward of
America's relationship with its Muslim citizens.

Dr. Reza deals with the politics of the day, the Islamophobes, and
has something to say about the Israel-Palestine conflict. If you are
interested in reading a great account of what's been happening over
the past decade and a half you need to read this book.
If you are interested in repairing the seared image of Muslims in
your community you need to begin to duplicate what has been done
in Connecticut. I have personally used many of the strategies
discussed in my community in New York and can bear witness that
they really work! The Islamophobes will not be able to win if you
(Muslims) just get involved in your communities and not be
exclusivist!

Dr. Reza shows that he is not just a cardiologist dealing with
physical hearts, but he also deals with spiritual and social hearts!
He also demonstrates that he is truly a religious man that takes his
religion very seriously. He also shows that true Muslim men have
no problem with their wives being out in the forefront. Dr. Reza and
his wife Aida are great examples of a couple who genuinely want
good in their communities, thus they are involved with giving a lot
back to the community in which they live and work.

I recommend this book to you with no hesitation or equivocation; it
will be worth your time.

Dr. Reza, thank you for taking the time out of your already super
busy schedule to write this book. I believe it is very timely.

Yours in firm faith

Imam Dr. Salahuddin M. Muhammad
Imam Emeritus – Newburgh masjid
Newburgh, New York.

Stigmatized:

From 9/11 to Trump and Beyond
-An American Muslim Journey

Dr. Reza Mansoor

TABLE OF CONTENTS:

Stigmatized: From 9/11 to Trump and Beyond – An American Muslim Journey

Introduction   page 1
Chapter 1: The Shock of 9/11   page 5
Chapter 2: My Early Upbringing   page 9
Chapter 3: Pursuing the American Dream   page 19
Chapter 4: The Clash of Weak Scholarship   page 27
Chapter 5: The Aftermath of 9/11   page 33
Chapter 6: Challenges Emerge   page 43
Chapter 7: Abandoning the Constitution   page 53
Chapter 8: The Tail That Wags the Dog   page 65
Chapter 9: Spreading Fear   page 73
Chapter 10: Delegitimizing and Stigmatizing   page 81
Chapter 11: The President of the United States   page 89
Chapter 12: Open Houses of Worship   page 97
Chapter 13: One Thousand Open Houses   page 107
Chapter 14: Doors Keep Opening   page 117
Chapter 15: Living Islam - Serving Humanity   page 123
Chapter 16: September 2010 and Park 51   page 129
Chapter 17: Taking a Stand in Hartford   page 137
Chapter 18: The Tenth Anniversary of 9/11   page 143
Chapter 19: Recognized by the Supreme Court   page 155
Chapter 20: Understanding the Hate Radicalizing Our Youth   page 165
Chapter 21: Spasms of Hate – More Radicalization   page 185
Chapter 22: The Europe we Fled   page 195
Chapter 23: Jewish/Muslim Relations   page 201
Chapter 24: The Extremist Challenge   page 211
Chapter 25: Charting Our Future Beyond the Golden Door   page 225

Appendix: Islam Explained

Chapter 1: Belief in Islam   page 235
Chapter 2: Worship Practices in Islam   page 243
Chapter 3: Jihad, Shariah, and Other Misconceptions   page 249
Chapter 4: Muhammad the Messenger of God   page 261

I am dedicating this book to the youth of America of all faith communities that I trust will take us to a better place through education and the inspired values of understanding each other.

About the Author

Dr. Reza Mansoor is board certified in Internal Medicine and Cardiology and practices as a Cardiologist at Hartford Hospital.

He completed his medical degree from St. George's University School of Medicine in 1992. He completed his medical internship and residency at the University of Connecticut in Internal Medicine 1992-1995. He was a Chief Medical Resident at Hartford Hospital from 1995-1996 and received his Cardiology fellowship from the University of Connecticut from 1996-1999. He is an Assistant Clinical Professor of Medicine at the University Of Connecticut School Of Medicine.

Dr. Mansoor is President of the Islamic Association of Greater Hartford, Advisory Board Member of Muslim Student Association-CT Council, and Founding President of the Muslim Coalition of Connecticut. He is a past president of the Islamic Center of Connecticut and Islamic Council of New England.

He is actively involved in the inter-faith community and provides ongoing didactic presentations on Islam. He is First Vice-Chair of the Board of Trustees of Hartford Seminary and a former member of the Board of Trustees of Covenant Preparatory School in Hartford.

Acknowledgements

After God, the most loving and giving, there are a few people, without whose help, this book would not be possible. First and foremost my wife, Aida, has been a pillar of support and understanding. She has sacrificed a lot of our family time to be encouraging of this effort. Yasmin, my daughter and Yusuf, my son have also had to sacrifice their time with me, including vacation and relaxing family time, understanding my yearning to get this book complete. My sisters, Nasreen and Fahima have been a tower of support, pushing me to speed up my efforts and encouraging me to get the book completed.

There were three friends who edited this book and gave me very useful advice on writing and publishing this book. Ann Cronin, a retired Middle and High School English teacher, who has received national and statewide awards for her teaching and was awarded the 'Teacher of the Year', helped immensely in giving me ideas and helped in editing this book. Jeanne Thwaites, another award winning fiction writer helped in advising and editing the book. She won the University of California Berkeley's Eisner prize for prose literature in 1991 and 1992 and the Sri Lankan Gratiaen prize for creative writing in English in 1998. Both Ann and Jeanne's encouragement were a huge source of inspiration in difficult times. The last of the three friends is my son, Yusuf, a freshman at George Washington University; he was co-editor of his high school, Avon Old Farms "Winged Beaver" as well as being on the editorial team of his College, George Washington "Cherry Tree". His review and critique of the book was very helpful to me.

I would like to thank Naveed Imshad for the cover picture photography.

INTRODUCTION

After 63 years of delivering his message, Prophet Muhammad gave this, his last sermon on the plain of Arafat, in present day Saudi Arabia, during his last and only pilgrimage - the Hajj:

After praising, and thanking Allah (the One God), he said:

"O People, lend me an attentive ear, for I know not whether after this year, I shall ever be amongst you again. Therefore listen to what I am saying to you very carefully and take these words to those who could not be present here today.

O People, just as you regard this month, this day, this city as sacred, so regard the life and property of every Muslim as a sacred trust. Return the goods entrusted to you to their rightful owners. Hurt no one so that no one may hurt you. Remember that you will indeed meet your Lord, and that He will indeed hold you accountable for your deeds. God has forbidden you from taking usury (interest), therefore all interest obligation shall henceforth be waived. Your capital, however, is yours to keep. You will neither inflict nor suffer any inequity. God has judged that there shall be no interest and that all the interest due to Abbas ibn 'Abd'al Muttalib (the prophet's uncle) shall henceforth be waived...

Beware of Satan, for the safety of your religion. He has lost all hope that he will ever be able to lead you astray in big things, so beware of following him in small things.

O people, it is true that you have certain rights with regard to your women, but they also have rights over you.

Remember that you have taken them as your wives only under God's trust and with His permission. If they abide by your right then to them belongs the right to be fed and clothed in kindness. Treat your women well and be kind to them for they are your partners and committed helpers. And it is your right that they do not make friends with any one of whom you do not approve, as well as never to be unchaste.

O People, listen to me in earnest, worship God, perform your five daily prayers (Salah), fast during the month of Ramadan, and give of your wealth in Zakat (poor due). Perform Hajj (the pilgrimage) if you can afford to.

All mankind is from Adam and Eve, an Arab has no superiority over a non-Arab and a non-Arab has no superiority over an Arab; a white person has no superiority over a black person and a black person has no superiority over a white person, except by piety and good action. Learn that every Muslim is a brother to every Muslim and that the Muslims constitute one brotherhood. Nothing shall be legitimate to a Muslim which belongs to a fellow Muslim unless it was given freely and willingly. Do not, therefore, do injustice to yourselves.

Remember, one day you will appear before God and answer for your deeds. So beware, do not stray from the path of righteousness after I am gone.

O people, no prophet or apostle will come after me and no new faith will be born. Reason well, therefore, O people, and understand these words which I convey to you. I leave behind me two things, the Qur'an (divine revelation) and my example, the Sunnah and if you follow these you *will never go astray.*

All those who listen to me should pass on my words to others and those to others again; and may the last ones understand my words better than those who listen to me directly. Be my witness, O God, that I have conveyed your message to your people".

This was the sermon Prophet Muhammad (On whom be peace) made after the conquest of Makkah, when he was the undisputed leader of the Arabian Peninsula, on his final and only Hajj pilgrimage. A few months later he would be dead.

Read it again...no Arab exceptionalism, no gloating over his victories, just a very humble plea to his followers to be aware of their responsibilities to each other, to gender equity, to financial fairness and responsibility, and a plea to be just, as this life is a trust from God and to Him we will all return.

This speech is regarded as a summary statement of the prophet's teachings. It gives you a flavor of what a just and fair leader he was to all.

For a Muslim, disregarding these words is very serious. Each major religion always has renegade extremists and we have had ours, but to judge all Muslims by those who have gone off the rails is to ignore why one fourth of the world population has chosen to follow the Prophet's teaching.

Reza Mansoor

Chapter 1

The Shock of 9/11

September 11th 2001, was a beautiful sunny day in New York and it was the same in Wethersfield, Connecticut where I lived. I am a cardiologist and started my day, as usual, by seeing the sickest of my hospitalized patients.

One of them was a young man with Amyloid cardiomyopathy, a devastating illness that, in its most aggressive form, can be rapidly fatal, as it was to be in the case of this young man. As I walked into his room that day I looked at his television screen and saw a plane hitting the second World Trade Center tower.

I felt sick to my stomach as I realized that this could not be the act of a lone madman but had to be the plot of many people acting with coordination and premeditation. My immediate thoughts were that a hostile group was trying to send a message to the people of the United States and I hoped it was not misguided Muslims that had carried out this act of terror.

Worse news followed. As the day went on we found out that both Trade Center towers had collapsed, killing thousands of people. To my horror, it was later broadcast that a group claiming to be behind the disaster also claimed to be Muslim. It was numbing to imagine that people who believe in God would, in their wildest dreams, think that God would sanction or condone this awful act of carnage.

I am a devout Muslim, a follower of Islam, and I know that such violence is counter to the very basics of our faith. Whatever your reason, you cannot use means that are against the basic principles of Islam to attain your goal. The means and the results must always be pure. The killing of innocent civilians is *NEVER* permissible.

As a physician I felt especially outraged, as did the other American Muslims in the medical profession whom I spoke to. Full 10% of America's physicians are Muslim and we spend all our working time and effort in trying to save lives, on a daily basis. We try so hard to save a single life and now, on our television screens, we were looking at an appalling act of devastation of human life and the commentators now kept attributing this to Muslim terrorists and, by inference, to Islam as well.

I could not get away from the horror of this act! They just kept replaying the images and everyone was glued to their television screens. Each time I walked past a screen it was the same devastating images and each time there was a little more information as the details of the attack became known. Each time they showed the devastation, people got angrier.

This disaster came to be called 9/11. The ramifications of this act of terror and its aftermath would affect us, the American Muslim community, disproportionately, for years to come, and still does, fifteen years on. Many Muslims in the United States began to be viewed and treated with great suspicion and in some instances were viewed as traitors to our own country; all based on a few very misguided deviants of our faith and lots of stereotyping by some outside of our faith.

An act of this magnitude shows a complete abandonment of God. If you act out on every injustice outside the parameters of the laws established to guide you, and you break God's laws to carry out retribution for what you think is an injustice, then you are outside the fold of civilized humanity and certainly outside the fold of Islam and its guiding rules for a humane society.

Going through that day was very tough. At work I overheard people making comments such as "We should nuke their holy sites", referring to Makkah and Medina. They were almost blind to the fact that there were adherents of Islam who valued these holy sites that were saving lives in the very hospital they worked in. An act of depravity by a few was resulting in judgment being passed on all adherents of Islam. Anger and revenge was on the mind of many, but most people had genuine questions "Why did they do this to us? What were their grievances? What part of the world were they from?" And inevitably, "what was their religion?"

This was a wound that would take a long time to heal.

In Connecticut, over the last decade and a half, we found a way to overcome some of the mistrust and to be seen as healers. It took a long time and a lot of courage and required us to go out of our comfort zone, but it was done. I would like to tell you that story and the positive steps that paid dividends in return. It is a journey that led us to the Supreme Court of Connecticut to collect an award for outreach and education on Law Day - May 1st 2013.

The organization we started in the ashes of 9/11, the Muslim Coalition of Connecticut (MCCT), was created to overcome the hate caused by people thousands of miles away who gave in to their frustrations and, despite religion, committed this most hateful act. This was the organization that was being recognized for its efforts at building bridges where walls of distrust existed. It is a model I wish I could export to all parts of our troubled nation. In writing this book my intension is very much to show that through sincere efforts and honest outreach we can overcome, in fact, we must overcome the fear and mistrust of each other that today plagues our nation with no sign of ending.

Let me start with the story of how I came to this country that I proudly call my home.

Chapter 2

My Early Upbringing

I was born in Colombo, the capital of Sri Lanka, a very beautiful small island that lies off the southern coast of India. Like the United States of America, the island of Sri Lanka, formerly Ceylon, was a British Colony. The U.S. broke free of Britain in 1776 and 172 years later, in 1948, Ceylon also became independent and became known as the Democratic Socialist Republic of Sri Lanka.

There are four main ethnic groups in Sri Lanka, each with a different major religion:

1. The Sinhalese majority are mostly Buddhists.
2. The Tamils, the largest minority, are mostly Hindus.
3. Muslims or followers of Islam.
4. Dutch Burghers (descendants from European settlers) are mostly Christians of various denominations.

Today, most educated urban Sri Lankans speak English and at least one of the two other local languages Sinhala and Tamil; languages with different roots and scripts. We spoke English to each other at home and Tamil and Sinhala with our friends.

Apart from an occasional flaring up of ethnic tensions, the majority Buddhist community and the minority Muslim community have got on very well. Muslims have been represented in government since Sri Lanka's independence from Britain. However, from 1983 to 2009 the Sinhala speaking Buddhist majority and the Tamil speaking Hindu minority were locked in a horrendous civil war. Diversity of races, languages and religions can be used to create dissension and disunity when politicians, and sometimes even religious leaders, want to exaggerate differences among groups to further their individualistic political goals. That is exactly what had happened in Sri Lanka.

I was the youngest in a family with three siblings. My Muslim family was upper middle class. My father, Fayesz, was a businessman, and my mother, Niloufer, was the director of a nursing home. My maternal grandfather, Dr. Kaleel, was a physician and a cabinet minister in the second government after Sri Lanka became independent of England.

In the 1970s I listened avidly to the events that led up to the civil war in Sri Lanka. They were the subject of many of our family's discussions. The origin of the conflict had started a long time prior, and was driven by opportunistic politicians using religious and ethnic differences to stoke up fear, while promising a false ethnic panacea by scapegoating minorities.

In 1956, Mr. Bandaranaike became Prime Minister by promising to replace English with Sinhala as the official language, using religion (Buddhism) to promote his agenda during his election campaign. He was not the most popular candidate, and his party was not the most popular party, until he started his campaign for Sinhala as the official language. His popularity soared after that and he won a landslide election. The minority communities felt dispossessed by this act and so the seeds of ethnic tension were sown. His political party, the Sri Lankan Freedom Party had captured the Sinhala speaking Buddhist majority on a 'nationalist' platform. But nationalism when used by politicians to favor one religion or ethnic group, and invariably stigmatize a minority, should be seen as thinly veiled racism. It seems to appeal to some who don't have a wide vision of the consequences that follow.

The seeds of hatred and ethnic tension once started are not easily controlled or quelled. Once the genie is out of the bottle it is impossible to get it back in.

Bandaranaike was assassinated in 1959 by a Buddhist monk. His wife, Sirimavo, contested the position of Prime Minister and became the first woman head of government in the world. Unfortunately, she continued his policies of ethnic isolation of minorities by the 'Sinhala Only Act'. Many political leaders who followed played their part in fomenting the tension that ultimately led to the civil war in Sri Lanka.

One element of this policy was the introduction of Sinhala as the national language of Sri Lanka, including in the school system. Being the youngest member of my family I was the only person made to study Sinhala as my first language. This was hard for me in the beginning, as everyone at home spoke English, but I realized the value of learning two languages. The most challenging part was that all the other subjects were also taught in a language that I was only just beginning to learn.

As much of Sri Lanka and the world still used English, my parents were very concerned that studying in Sinhala, I would not be able to compete in higher education or for employment. Therefore at the age of thirteen my mother decided it would be better to send me to study in England.

I had to relearn everything in English, including mathematical and scientific terms that I knew only in Sinhala, a language that has its roots in Sanskrit, an ancient Indian language, with a totally different script. Three years later, I had to take the standardized British 'ordinary level' examinations, competing with students throughout the world. It was a nightmare; adjusting to a new country, a new language, and having to cope with the pressure of all the examinations so soon.

By the time I was a teenager I had learned a lot about the constant nature of change. I could not help but wonder, however, at the devastating effect a politician's ambitiousness in wanting to get elected, and using language and religion as political tools, had made.

The unfortunate consequences of political opportunists I would see time and again throughout the world. They usually precede civil wars, apartheid regimes, ethnic cleansing or even genocide because the use of religion and nationalism are potent tools and, in the wrong hands, can have devastating effects. Unfortunately, they do serve short term political goals.

I was in England for five years and did the 'ordinary level' and two years later, the 'advanced level' examinations. I did not do well enough as a 'foreign student' to get into a medical school in United Kingdom as there were restricted openings for foreign students in the U.K.

My father suggested I apply to medical schools in Sri Lanka as they all taught in English. Imagine the upheaval the change in a national language had brought to students who had stayed in Sri Lanka and studied in Sinhala for all those years. They now had to switch to English for higher studies. They had become guinea pigs forced to endure the consequences of a careless political decision.

My mother disagreed with my father's suggestion. She said that our country and its education system was a mess and the civil war, which had begun in 1983, meant that there was too much instability in the system. But I really wanted to come home and not have to repeat my exams in the hope of getting a better score in order to enter a medical school in the U.K. Based on my results; I was admitted to North Colombo Medical College, a new private medical school in Sri Lanka. This tipped the scale and I returned home to Sri Lanka.

I loved being back, did well in my work and had a great group of friends at school. Knowing the difficulties we were going through as a nation, in the middle of a civil war, made us take our studies all the more seriously. We enjoyed working hard.

Prashanth was one of my best friends. He was a Sri Lankan Tamil who had lost his father at a young age. His father was always his role model. His father was a doctor and Prashanth wanted to follow in his footsteps. He was a friend of mine from my early days in Prep School, before I went to England, and now he was in medical school with me. We did lots of studying but also had lots of fun together.

Sumith was another very good friend. A Sinhalese Buddhist, whose father was a surgeon and was practicing in the war ravaged north of the country. He would often relate gory details of the surgeries he got to watch his father perform. Sumith was probably one of the most brilliant students I have ever met. In addition to his academic achievements, he would challenge medical students to play chess with him and he played and won without even looking at the chess board. He memorized the positions of each piece on the chess board and played by telling a person, acting as his player, where to move each chess piece while looking in the opposite direction to the board. It was amazing to watch.

My mother was right. After two years the civil war took a turn for the worse. Our medical school was blown up by an extreme Sinhalese political group that was upset at the government negotiating with the Tamils in the north. The bombing took place in 1987 and was just prior to the 2nd MB (Bachelor of Medicine) national pre-clinical (pre-hospital) examination. That was the end of medical studies in Sri Lanka for me.

The medical school was closed for over two years. I applied to dozens of medical schools all over the world but heard nothing. The longer I was out of school the dimmer got my chances of continuing my medical studies. No school wants to take a student who had been out of school for two years. Furthermore, no medical school would take a student from a school that no longer existed. The British body that recognizes medical schools had decided to take North Colombo Medical College off their list of recognized medical schools.

This challenging two year period ended for me during the month of Ramadan, the month of fasting for Muslims and, one of the most spiritual in the Muslim calendar year. In my most desolate time alone in prayer I would pray for my studies to resume. It became a daily prayer often culminating in tears at everything falling apart, or so it seemed to me at that time.

Soon after the month of Ramadan my prayers were miraculously answered. I was offered a scholarship to St. George's University School of Medicine in Grenada and, the real prospect of clinical or hospital training in the United States of America.

Almost immediately after that I got a letter saying that I had been granted a full tuition and board scholarship to Kalikut Medical College in Kerala, India. I did not accept the latter as I had already been offered my dream. Medical training in the United States of America was that dream.

Everyone knew America was the best place to get 'state of the art' training in the latest that medical science had to offer. It was also a dreamland where everyone had freedom and opportunity, as long as they were willing to work hard. I was thrilled.

At that time, prior to its collapse, the Soviet Union together with the eastern bloc countries were in competition with the western world in trying to woo small countries like Sri Lanka. Both sides wanted to form exclusive relationships with developing nations. In Sri Lanka some political parties were being wooed by the Communist nations and so had close associations with them, but the ordinary people were far more in support of 'The West', particularly the United States of America, and everything it stood for.

Some of my fellow students went to Eastern European countries such as Bulgaria and even to Russia. Sumith and his girl friend went to Bulgaria. They learned a new language and medicine at the same time. Others got opportunities in India, Australia and Cuba, but the dream was to get to America.

When I told my friends in medical school that I had been accepted into a medical school in Grenada, with the possibility of doing my clinical training in the United States, they were in awe. It was not so much because I was resuming my medical studies but that I had the opportunity to do my clinical or hospital training in the United States.

Part of the allure of course was Hollywood that had created this magical land of complete freedom and opportunity. Those who had been there, my mother included, had stories of a land of amazing things. America had oversized candy, fantastic varieties of ice cream, and delicious fast food outlets. There was plenty of everything. That at least was the perception I had had as a child and that was what stuck. As I grew older what appealed to me, more and more, was the opportunity that we heard the U.S. allowed its entire population. You could be what you wanted to be through hard work and live out your dream; it was called 'the American dream'.

The same economic opportunities that had been the key attraction for the colonists, who had immigrated to the American continent centuries ago, were still a key attraction. Today immigrants still come to seek a better tomorrow.

What a contrast that was to what we heard about the Soviet Union. That was a country which was managed by the State, spying was the norm, and the KGB, its main security agency, was everywhere, monitoring everything. Who wants to go to a nation where the government spies on its citizens' personal lives? The idea was abhorrent to all. In my mind, the land of freedom and opportunity easily won out against a land of excessive security, state control and meddling!

Chapter 3

Pursuing the American Dream

In December of 1990, after my pre-clinical (pre-hospital) training in Grenada in the West Indies, I started clinical (hospital) training in Coney Island Hospital in Brooklyn, New York.

After studying in two tropical islands I was in for a shock. Not only was Coney Island not an island, but it was the end of December and it was the height of winter. I could only dream of the beautiful tropical islands I had left behind.

I arrived at John F. Kennedy International Airport with dreams of training hard to be the best physician I could. Then reality hit! I was in danger of freezing to death! New York City was huge and icy cold even to the eye. It had tall concrete buildings and its people were all wrapped up in dark clothes and were very unfriendly at first. This is what winter in New York City felt like to a new comer.

But it was only the climate that was painful. I quickly found out that I had many Sri Lankan medical student friends at the hospital, who had preceded me to the U.S.A. Renza and Joshua were two seniors in medical school in Sri Lanka and offered to keep me in their house till I found a place of my own. Renza was a Sri

Lankan Muslim, who had lived most of his youth in Canada, and Joshua was half Jewish and half Tamil. As they had come before me they showed me what I had to do to get by. They were both helpful and welcoming. They were already doing their clinical training in Coney Island Hospital in Brooklyn where I was to start in January and they knew the ropes.

One of the first things they taught me was that once you find a cheap apartment, close to the hospital, you have to go for a long walk and find furniture that was discarded by others. You have to let other students know the location of it and they would transport it to your apartment. It is exactly what I did knowing all too well what germs and worse could be on the furniture and mattresses I found. These are life's requirements that students in faraway lands from their home had to endure.

Coney Island Hospital in downtown Brooklyn was in a run-down area. It was a large inner city hospital and was known for its excellent training programs in Medicine, Surgery, Pediatrics, and Obstetrics and Gynecology; the main disciplines required to pass the core curriculum in clinical training. It was a very busy hospital and the training I received was outstanding.

I noticed right from the start that in the United States you get credit for how hard you worked and not so much for who you are. Religion and ethnic origin did not play much of a role in how you rose academically. The British, on the other hand, had seen me as a foreigner first. This was not so in the U.S. and I attributed the difference to the fact that the U.S. was founded by a melting pot of immigrants. All but Native Americans and those African Americans who are descended from slaves, had ancestors who had come to the U.S. looking for a better life, from some other country. It was therefore not a big deal to be different in skin color and accent, especially in Brooklyn. Although other nations are proud of their supposed meritocracy, to me, the U.S. is unique in its embrace of hard work and real meritocracy.

I enjoyed my training in Coney Island Hospital and learned a lot about the practice of medicine in the 'New World'. I did my core clinical rotations and my sub-specialty 'electives' from December 1990 to June 1992, when I graduated. Because the hospital was located in a run-down area we had to be careful getting around, especially at night. There was heavy drug addiction and, as a result, a lot of petty crime.

Joshua and Renza, the two friends who had helped me so much when I initially came to America, had both been assaulted and pistol whipped and their possessions taken from them while walking close to the hospital at night. As a result, when we were applying for residency training, which is after graduation from medical school, most of us chose to leave Brooklyn. I interviewed widely and was accepted by my first choice, the University of Connecticut Health Center residency training program in Farmington, Connecticut.

I loved Farmington in particular and Connecticut in general for its greenery, beauty and quiet. New York was too loud and busy for me and there was too much violence in Brooklyn. Most of all, the

University of Connecticut is what I now consider American medicine at its best. Respect for patient's rights and their privacy were taken to a much higher level of consideration here, as was respect for trainees' needs. In this it was very different from Coney Island Hospital, where we learned a lot about medicine but the privacy and respect for the individual was lacking.

There was a big change in my life in 1992. When I graduated, I got married to Aida, who joined me from England and became my partner in everything I did thereafter. Since I was changing status from student to resident trainee, I could not leave the country. As a result our families came down to Texas, where my uncle lived, and we got married in a wonderful simple wedding ceremony. It was very different from the huge and expensive weddings of Sri Lanka, but I liked it all the more for that simplicity.

I had gotten to know Aida in England when I was a teenager. She cared deeply for humanitarian issues and yearned to stand up against injustice. She would often ask me "Do you think we would have stood up against Nazism if we lived in that time?"

From the age of five to nine Aida had lived in Zambia and never lost her deep love for Africa and its people. She protested against the South African apartheid regime by standing vigil outside its London embassy in Trafalgar Square, and would tell me all about her activism, even after I had left Sri Lanka.

I respected her immensely for her sense of justice and her calm demeanor, and dreamed of having a person like her in my life to walk with, in this constantly challenging and changing life journey. When I went back to Sri Lanka to continue my studies I missed Aida and the discussions we had had. She wanted us to play a role in bringing positive change in the world while embracing life's hurdles. When my studies ground to a halt due to the civil war in Sri Lanka, it became difficult to keep that positive view of life and speaking to Aida on the phone gave me immense encouragement.

Once I got admission to St. George's Medical School in Grenada to continue my studies, I asked my parents to allow me to get engaged to Aida. They agreed, and on my way to Grenada in the West Indies, in 1989, we all stopped off in England and had a small engagement ceremony. When we got married, in 1992, I was twenty-five and Aida was twenty-four.

In Connecticut, I became aware that most non-Muslims in the U.S. knew very little about Islam. For example, when we were expecting our first child Yasmin, in 1995, Aida decided to wear the 'hijab', or headscarf, as a sign of the modesty that Islam encouraged, a decision that was entirely hers, as it should be. However, we found that many Americans thought the 'hijab' is a male-enforced garment and that it is a part of Islamic doctrine that a husband entirely controls his wife by. This is of course entirely false.

Aida liked to say "The 'hijab' is a statement that I value my spirituality and intellect above my looks, which are often used as marketing tools to objectify me". "It is a reflection of my Islamic feminism" she would often say.

I was, therefore, totally taken aback when I was asked by a professor in the residency-training program "Why do you make your wife wear that thing on her head?" She did not ask me why she wore it; she just jumped to the conclusion that I had made her wear it. Also referring to the hijab as 'that thing' is derogatory. Would a catholic nun's head gear or 'habit' similarly have been a tool for insulting her with?

In the U.S., women who wear the 'hijab' do so of their own free will. There is an active debate among Muslim women on its importance. Some hold that it is mandatory and others that the Qur'an demands only modesty. What is not allowed is the enforcement of something in religion on another person, as the Qur'an states in 2:256 **"Let there be no compulsion in religion because truth stands out clear from error"**.

We started life in Connecticut by living in a small one bedroom rented apartment in New Britain. We had one car and we were content in our simple lifestyle. Internship and residency training in medicine was hard work and I was learning so much that I hardly had time for anything else. Both Aida's father and brother had trained as physicians in England, so I had a life partner who understood my struggle in training and this made a big difference to me. She was empathic when I came home tired and always had a warm smile and warm meal to welcome me.

I did well in my residency training and was offered the position of Chief Medical Resident at Hartford Hospital, an honor reserved for the two best medical residents per hospital. I very much enjoyed the challenge and trust that was placed in me as a teacher, administrator, and student, all at the same time, as I was in charge of all the medical residents and their training.

Chapter 4

The Clash of Weak Scholarship

In 1995, my year as a Chief Medical Resident at Hartford Hospital, I started getting more involved in the Muslim community. It was at that time that I began to appreciate the extent of misunderstanding about Islam that existed in America.

In 1993 Samuel Huntington had written the 'Clash of Civilizations', a theory first introduced in 1990 by Bernard Lewis in his article 'The Roots of Muslim Rage' in *The Atlantic*. The Clash of Civilizations is a theory that suggested that people's cultural and religious identities would be the primary source of conflict in the post-Cold War world. It was based on some major misunderstandings.

Both writers saw the Muslim world and 'The West' as incompatible forces pitted against each other. Lewis's article examined the 1977 Iranian revolution and its political aftermath. He had come to the conclusion that the hostage crisis was caused by Iranian anger against America, but had then extrapolated that to suggest that this had to do with their religion as Muslims. This was incorrect. He had converted a political conflict into a religious one with no evidence to point to that conclusion.

The Iranian conflict had begun in 1953 with the installation of Shah Reza Pahlavi against the elected Iranian government of Mosaddeqh in a CIA inspired coup. Many Iranians were angry at the persistent support the United States had given the increasingly despotic Shah.

To conflate this political drama with a 'Clash of Civilizations' between Islam and 'The West' is obviously trying to make a fact fit a theory, and in this case it did not fit.

4.6% of Muslims live in Iran. So how does a political conflict involving a minute Muslim population of the world suddenly become his reason for the clash theory he proposes for all Muslims? It is based on weak scholarship and flawed reasoning.

Lewis also explains Christendom's separation of church and state came from Jesus' saying "give unto Caesar what is Caesar's, give unto God what is God's." He says Islam has no such separation. Again his scholarship is weak. In Islam there was a perfect example of separation of religion and state in the 'Constitution of Medina' which was drafted by Prophet Mohammad in approximately 622 C.E. If Lewis had examined that document he would have found that the Prophet supported the separation of religion and state. The Constitution of Medina considered the rights of Jews (because there was a sizeable population of Jews in Medina), Christians, non-believers and all other minorities who were part of the *Ummah* (community). It supported religious rights and freedoms for all minorities, barred any violence in Medina, set agreements on tribal relations, addressed the rights and protection of women and included a taxation system.

It required that everyone was to participate in the protection of Medina, but if there was an attack on Islam, only Muslims were responsible for defending their religion. Others were not obligated to do so.

No constitution of this depth is known to have existed prior to Medina's. Yet Bernard Lewis ignored this very famous document or did not know about it when he wrote his article. Either way this points to poor scholarship.

In 1993, Samuel P. Huntington, a political scientist known for his analysis of the relationship between the military and the civil government, also wrote in *Foreign Affairs* that future world relations would be based on civilizational differences, pitting large civilizations against each other, and in particular Islam against Christianity. He contended that western values, such as individualism, liberalism, constitutionalism, human rights, equality, liberty, the rule of law, democracy, free markets, and separation of church and state, have little resonance in Islamic or other cultures.

Edward Said, who was a Christian Middle East scholar who taught at Columbia and Yale Universities and was a visiting professor at Harvard, Stanford and John Hopkins Universities, wrote in his book 'Orientalism' that certain people believe that others' appearance, skin and hair color, religions, languages, clothing, cultures etcetera are inferior to their own, just because they themselves happen to be in the group in power, referring to Huntingdon's absurd assertion that basic rights are somehow western values. He called Huntingdon's opinions, 'The Clash of Ignorance'.

This ignorance among non-Muslim academics, when they referred to us, was something I would see repeatedly. First it was by university academics and after 9/11 by others that suddenly became scholars or experts without any true academic scholarship. 'Terrorism experts' sprouted everywhere and they were Middle East experts as well as experts on Islam, but they all had an agenda of pitting Islam against 'The West'. They often referred to the self fulfilling 'Clash of Civilizations' theory as a potent alibi for their fears.

Many of these 'scholars' declare they are authorities on subjects they have little knowledge about. The message of these self proclaimed experts, broadcast in the media, sent shock waves in the Muslim community. Everything ended the same way – there is a clash and they hoped that if they repeated it frequently enough people would believe them.

Of course I am not accusing all non-Muslims of ignorance when they write about us. David Brooks of the *New York Times* wrote, "after the Arab uprisings which began in Tunisia and extended across the Middle East, that Huntington's claim that the Muslim culture was inhospitable to democracy and pluralism has been proven wrong"[1]. Brooks highlighted Huntington's shoddy scholarship, especially when it comes to understanding 'the other'.

Huntington also ignored the fact that Muslims, like myself, are immigrating to the United States in large numbers because this country is not in conflict with Islamic values at all.

Furthermore, we are not monolithic. Islam spans the globe with 1.6 billion followers. You will be hard pressed to find a single country where there are no Muslims. As a result you will find very divergent opinions among us about almost every subject.

Arab and Muslim do not mean the same thing, despite the frequent stereotypes. There are over 100 million Muslims in China, which is more than in Saudi Arabia, Syria and Iraq together. Indonesia, the country with the largest Muslim population has over 200 million Muslims and they are not Arabs. The next 3 most populous countries of Muslims are Pakistan, India and Bangladesh – none of them are Arab speaking. I want you to understand the diversity of Muslims so that you understand that the stereotypes are completely inconsistent with reality.

The factor that is missing in clarifying who we are to Americans is ourselves. As Muslims, we have to immerse ourselves into this equation and the mis-portrayal of us and clarify and represent ourselves, not allowing others to do this for us through stereotyping us. For the sake of our nation's well being we have to change this narrative.

---

[1] http://www.nytimes.com/2011/03/04/opinion/04brooks.html

Chapter 5

The Aftermath of 9/11

"If anyone slew a person (unjustly), it would be as if he slew the whole of humanity and if anyone saved a life it would be as if he saved the life of the whole of humanity".

(Qur'an 5:32)

This verse had a profound effect on me when I was growing up and pulled at my heartstrings. To serve God you have to serve humanity. That is the calling of the Qur'an and played the most significant role in leading me to my ultimate profession as a physician.

What happened on 9/11 can never be understood from an Islamic perspective and we condemned it at every opportunity. I remember some Muslims taking full page ads in newspapers and listing all the scholars and organizations that had condemned this heinous act of terror.

Immediately after 9/11 I wrote a 'letter to the editor' at the *Hartford Courant* explaining that Islam does not in any way condone acts of terrorism and the killing of innocents. Our guidance does not come from any individual call to violence. Our guidance comes from the *Qur'an* and the prophet's teachings and example (*Sunnah*) calling to a path of peace and serenity both within oneself and within the community at large (see appendix section on Islam at the end). Both these sources, the *Qur'an* and the *Sunnah*, bear witness to the fact that what was done on that horrible day had nothing to do with the religion of Islam.

What was crazy was that while we spoke out, media 'pundits' were declaring that Muslims who did not believe in violence were silent. As though there was no moderate voice in Islam, or worse, that we were all part of a conspiracy to bring 'The West' down and were therefore quiet. They asked, "Where is the moderate voice?" or "why aren't moderate Muslims speaking out?" "How come we never hear Muslims condemning what was done on 9/11." When we invited the media to our interfaith gatherings when we did speak out and clarify the Muslim position, we would get the "Sorry, this is not newsworthy" response. It was a classic catch-22 situation. You can't hear the moderate voice if you refuse to listen.

At that time I realized that non-Muslims longed to find out the truth about us for themselves and also wanted to know more about Islam. Qur'an's were flying off the shelves and people were enrolling in classes to learn more about Islam.

To answer this need I called on many of the scholars in the area, including Dr. Ingrid Mattson, a professor of Islam and Christian Muslim relations at Hartford Seminary, local Imams (prayer leaders) and students of Islam who readily agreed to write articles clarifying our faith. I made a list of topics and asked each to write an article on one of them. We covered topics like the basics of Islam, the concept of Jihad, women in Islam, the family unit in Islam, and the Islamic view on justice. These were the areas that non-Muslims had the most questions about – and I clarify all these topics at the end of this book in the Appendix.

On October 21st, a little over a month after 9/11, the articles were published in the editorial section of the Hartford Courant under the title "Understanding Islam"[2],[3] and these articles covered most of that section of the paper. Most people appreciated what we were doing and, to this day, this series of articles is being used in religious diversity classes to explain our faith.

There was however a pervading fear, in the Muslim community, that there would be a backlash against Muslims due to the terrorist attacks of 9/11. Muslim leaders began to call community members advising us, especially women, to stay indoors and keep a low profile. As I was a physician I couldn't afford that luxury. However, at work, many people from nurses to doctors to laborers in the hospital came up to me and asked me whether I was all right. They could sense the anguish I felt. Their kindness gave me a sense of belonging to this country.

My family and I never felt personally insecure during this time. We had so many friends and acquaintances that called and asked us if everything was okay. They asked if they could accompany us to the malls or grocery stores. We even got flowers from neighbors

---

[2] http://articles.courant.com/2001-10-21/news/0110210790_1_understanding-islam-status-of-muslim-women-koran
[3] http://articles.courant.com/2001-10-21/news/0110210789_1_understanding-islam-solidarity-status-of-muslim-women

with letters wishing us well and sent to the mosque. The memory of that open affection and love is something I cherish to this day.

On September 15th 2001, the Saturday after 9/11, St. Mary's church in Newington, a suburb of Hartford, wanted a Muslim who could speak at a Memorial Service for the victims of the attacks. The Hartford Seminary asked me if I would do it. Although to speak publicly was very difficult at this time, I agreed, and my wife and I went to the church.

When the congregation saw Aida, with her head covered, there was pin-drop silence. It was probably the most difficult public speech I have ever made. But I had prepared and practiced it many times and the words came from my heart. I explained my devastation, both as a physician and a Muslim, at seeing the carnage brought about by people claiming to be Muslims. What they did was incompatible with being a Muslim.

After my speech I could see relief on the part of the audience. I stopped at the exit because a very long line of people was waiting to speak to me. They wished us well and many gave me small American flags which they had been given at the entrance to the event, as a mark of appreciation for my coming. They commended my bravery in speaking out and attested that my message was deeply appreciated. I also got a message on my answer phone at home from a veteran of the US army who did not leave his name or number but said "Doctor, I heard you speak and if you get any trouble I want you to know we have your back. You were sincere and I know that." That simple act was immensely reassuring. So, despite what some in the media were saying, as individuals, people seemed to be ignoring the messages of fear.

It wasn't like this everywhere. A Sikh, Balbir Singh Sodhi, was killed on that very same day in Mesa Arizona because he was wearing a turban and because Osama bin Laden, now reported to be the leader of Al-Qaeda, the organization behind the 9/11 terror attacks, wore a turban[4]. Sodhi had done nothing wrong. We heard that many Sikhs who wore turbans were now being targeted.

A federal government official report stated there had been a 1700% increase in "anti-Muslim" incidents. There had been twenty-eight hate incidents against Muslims in 2000 and 481 in 2001 and these were just the reported crimes. A large number of insults and violent hate acts went unreported.

This led to fear in the Muslim community but President George Bush went out of his way to explain the difference between the religion of Islam and the acts of terror, in my opinion, helping people understand us and alleviate tension considerably. He very clearly expressed that American Muslims should not be blamed for the act of a few terrorists.

Speaking to the Muslims he said *"We respect your faith. It's practiced freely by millions of Americans and by many millions more in countries that America counts as friends. Its teachings are good and peaceful and those who commit evil in the name of Allah, blaspheme the name of Allah. The terrorists are traitors to their own faith, trying in effect to hijack Islam itself. The enemy of America is*

---

[4] http://www.harisingh.com/newsBacklash.htm

not our many Muslim friends. It is not our many Arab friends. Our enemy is a radical network of terrorists and every government that supports them." He said this on September 20th 2001.

What most people are unaware of is, that while in America Muslims are 1% of the population, about 10% of all U.S. physicians is Muslim. That means that a large part of our minority American Muslim community consists of physicians whose chosen job is to heal and save lives. Most Americans, I am sure, have been treated by a Muslim physician sometime without their even knowing it. Contrast this to the stereotype of Muslims in America.

In November 2001 Garrett Condon, a reporter for the Hartford Courant, invited several Muslim physicians, including myself, to a discussion[5]. During that discussion we expressed that as physicians the association with terror hurt the most. We are so involved, as a consequence of our religious upbringing, in valuing life and the saving of it. How our religion can be portrayed through acts of terrorism was unfathomable.

I will always be grateful to the many Americans, particularly my patients, who reassured me as they understood how involved I was in the community. They would say things like "Most new immigrant groups go through a phase of not being accepted. Don't worry this will pass". However, I had to face the fact that other immigrant groups did not have the handicap of being associated with a terrorist act like 9/11. Hearing afterwards that there was

---

[5] http://articles.courant.com/2001-11-10/news/0111101152_1_muslim-islamic-faith-physicians

going to be a war to avenge that act of terror, was very disheartening. Wars have a habit of making things worse.

On October 14th 2001, an article in *The Hartford Courant* sent shivers down our spine. It spoke about the possible detention of Muslim Americans if there was war. It quoted Jerry Kang, a law professor at UCLA, who said that although in the court of public opinion the detention of Japanese Americans had been repudiated a long time ago, it had been deemed 'good law', that is to say it was a law that had been deemed constitutional by the U.S. Supreme Court in 1944.

World War II was surely one of the darkest periods in American history and we were now hearing that if there was another war some of those now-accepted American injustices could be imposed on us. People say history repeats itself but aren't human beings supposed to learn from history? Isn't what was wrong at one time, regardless of whom the victims were, wrong at all times? 'Never again' should mean never again to anyone, ever.

As if to pacify us the article went on to say that although the wholesale internment of Arab Americans was improbable, the likelihood of selective restrictions on the liberty of Arab Americans could increase dramatically and legally if there was a further terrorist strike from abroad. There was a sense of deep concern in the community after this article.

A few days later another *Hartford Courant* reporter, Amy Pagnozzi, interviewed me about this article[6]. Her article commented on the level of concern that the previous article had caused. We now know that there was no internment of all Muslims but that does not diminish, in my memory, the fear we felt in those uncertain times. In retrospect it is easy to say that those who worried were merely over-anxious, but at that time the fear was genuine.

When ordinary Americans asked "Why do those Muslims abroad hate us so much?", when talking about those who had chosen to blow up the Twin Towers, the answer the Bush administration gave was "because they hate our values." Perhaps this was partly true as extremists on all sides over-emphasize the cultural differences and incompatibility between "us and them". For example, the United States is accused of lax morals and loose values as if the majority of people who live here are guilty of this. The emphasis on poor morals obviously comes from the way our television, movies and other media depict us. Millions here are straight-laced with the highest standards of morals and values. It was clear that we, the moderates everywhere, were in the passenger seat being taken for a ride by extremists everywhere.

In 2001 there were more challenges. According to a *Time* magazine poll in November, only 38% of the U.S. population claimed to personally know a Muslim, which meant 62% did not. Research shows that personal knowledge of others breaks down prejudice barriers, so this was a scary statistic to me. It meant that

---

[6] http://articles.courant.com/2001-10-16/news/0110160124_1_arab-americans-internment-military-necessity

the media could have an exaggerated effect in influencing public opinion, in their portrayal of Muslims.

The *Time* magazine article also stated that 17% of Americans that year held an unfavorable view of Muslims, a figure of around 60 million people, that we presumed was so high as a result of 9/11. That seemed logical as November 2001 was the height of the fear people had of Islam and Muslims and we hoped that would soon pass. Our work was clearly cut out for us. We had to have our neighbors know us better and reverse this statistic.

Chapter 6

Challenges Emerge

Muslims view the immediate post 9/11 period as a seminal moment. There was a vacuum in knowledge about us, as Muslims, that needed to be filled with real knowledge. We were being vilified based on the actions of a few misguided individuals and that needed to be clarified. The vast majority of American Muslims are dedicated to the betterment of this nation, the home in which we have chosen to live and bring up our children. I reiterate "chosen", since many American Muslims are immigrants or descendents of immigrants, and many chose to leave their countries of birth and come here based on a dream for a better future. That is 'the American dream', and it is alive and vibrant in the American Muslim community, the newest immigrants to our shores.

After 9/11, a cottage industry of self-styled 'scholars' of Islam emerged. Many were not Muslim, and knew very little about Islam, but didn't hesitate to write Op-Eds highlighting what they imagined Islam to be, and their theory on why Muslims carried out the acts of 9/11. In their Op-Eds they cherry picked verses of the Qur'an, quoting them out of context, painting Islam as a violent religion fixated on world domination.

They did not stop at there, they painted Islam as a very backward religion by attributing the worst cultural practices, that had nothing to do with Islam and were mostly banned by Islam, like female genital mutilation and honor killings, and somehow equated and blamed Islam for all of that. Not surprisingly some people got a very slanted view of Islam. These Op-Eds seemed to pop up everywhere.

The strength of Islam is in its encouragement to contribute fully to make the place you live in the best place it can possibly be, thus contributing to the betterment of society. I could not ignore my religious calling to write about what happened to us since 9/11 and help clarify many of the misconceptions. Muslims are striving to understand and address the fear that is being perpetuated, in the most positive of ways. We have no recourse even from a religious perspective but to face the fear mongering directly.

To understand this calling I would like to take you back to the initial call to prophet hood that Prophet Muhammad (on whom be peace) received at the age of forty. Revelation began to be received by him through arch-angel Gabriel, with these words:

> *"Read. Read in the name of your Lord who created,*
> *who created mankind from a clot.*
> *Read and your Lord is most generous.*
> *He is the One who taught by the use of the pen"*
> *Qur'an 96:1-4.*

To me this is a call to educate by the use of the pen. We must clarify and represent ourselves through God's given gift of communication and address misconceptions, particularly about our faith.

Since dehumanizing is the first step in stereotyping and vilifying us, I would like to humanize us, so let me tell you a little bit more about myself and my family.

Connecticut, where we live, is a state in the north-east of the United States, in what is called New England. The level of education, understanding and open-mindedness in this part of the nation has been exceptional. When there is a racist statement made by some public official, I find it difficult to find anybody I know who does not stand out strongly against this hatred. It has therefore encouraged me to be outspoken in clarifying Islam against those who spread fear.

One of our challenges living in New England has been coping with the harsh winters, but in the spring of 2012 when I began writing, we had had a mild winter, and as I complete this book in the spring of 2016 we had another mild winter.

Spring is a time of rebirth and renewal, a time to reflect and review our present state of affairs and determine the direction and path our nation should follow. There is a tussle between our nation's founding principles and a new fear based ideology that is creeping into our discourse that needs to be addressed head on.

It is no coincidence that I started and completed this book in presidential election years. The short reason for that is that the level of discourse gets to its lowest around this time. There are some very opportunistic politicians who will scapegoat and stereotype minorities to help them win votes. This has caused spasms of fear and hate to grip the country, usually at the expense of minorities, particularly Muslims. If nobody stands up and clarifies the truth of Islam, rather than the concocted crazy one you hear in the media, we are all doomed to indefinite hostility and none of us can afford that.

As you get to know me and my family you will realize that we are a typical family striving for the same things that other families in America strive for. I am a hospital and community based clinical cardiologist, which means that my patients are those that have acute and chronic heart disease and are often quite debilitated by it. I am blessed to love what I do and have enjoyed getting to know most of my patients on a personal level. Many have attended the talks and events that I have organized to help us all get to know each other better, which I will explain later in the book.

I am also blessed to have a loving family. Aida and I have been married for 20 years (in 2012) and she has been my soul mate in everything I have done. She has encouraged me to keep striving, while juggling everything we do, despite the very uphill struggle this sometimes entails.

We have two wonderful teenage children. I know wonderful and teen are usually oxymoronic, but our children are really the best I could have ever wanted. Our daughter, Yasmin, despite having Asperger's syndrome, a variation of Autism, is one of the most loving and giving people I know. I miss her love and warmth terribly when I am away from her. Yusuf, our son, is an exceptionally gifted student who effortlessly balances his Islamic identity and his love and pride in the United States. His favorite subject is American history and he reads voraciously about this country's struggle for independence, its birth, its laws, and the devastating Civil War. He has an encyclopedic knowledge of the lives and actions of all the presidents of the United States and often quizzes us on some esoteric fact about their lives

Obviously, heavy time constraints are placed on my family time due to my commitment to medicine as well as local affairs. Despite that, I feel a calling to write this book to share my experiences so that most Americans who do not know a Muslim can get to know one and the challenges therein. It is also written so that other Muslims who might be experiencing similar challenging situations may take solace and learn from our experience. It entails having the courage to speak out and represent ourselves in an organized and united way. We must do that because in the vacuum we leave, if we don't, there is some fear monger with an agenda speaking on our behalf.

I have had in many ways an idyllic life in America. It has therefore been sad to see friction develop between the Muslim community and our neighbors after 9/11. Some members of the media began to promote the idea that all Muslims are required by their religion to be potentially dangerous enemies to the peaceful people they are living amongst. In fact, Islam requires its followers to live in harmony together in the community. That means that any violent person who calls himself a Muslim, is a renegade to his/her faith.

I found myself directly involved in leadership roles, particularly through the Muslim Coalition of Connecticut and the Islamic Council of New England, which brought me in frequent contact with other Muslim leaders. These discussions gave me a unique perspective on the challenges being faced by Muslims, not just in Connecticut but across the country. Lack of education and misinformation about Islam were urgent priorities that needed addressing.

One accusation was that Muslims are being 'radicalized' from within the Muslim community in America and that militants lead eighty percent of the mosques in the United States. New York Representative Peter King, a Republican politician with an obvious bias, who didn't even have his staff investigate the credibility of his sources, blindly repeated this accusation.

King headed a congressional investigation on American Muslim's 'roots of radicalization'. He had picked people for his 'investigation' that had similar biases to his, who repeated these biases which caused even more confusion and fear in the public sphere. His was a totally inaccurate portrayal of Muslims in America. I know that because I live here and am involved in the mosques in this area. It is not the mosques that are radicalizing people, it is social media and the internet based hate groups, on all sides, that are doing that.

Unfortunately, most mosques were not involved in outreach to the extent that was needed and that made our job even more difficult. Some mosques had leaders that did not understand the value of outreach. Many of the Imams (prayer leaders) and presidents (lay leaders) of insular mosques came from overseas and did not understand the way the U.S. functioned. Some of these leaders did not know how to deal with politicians or the political process. Often their sermons lacked relevance and lacked information on how to handle the fragile situation we were facing.

Some Imams were extremely conservative in their outlook but that per se was not the issue. They were simply out of touch with their community's needs. This lack of outreach hurt us as it meant an opportunity at education was lost. Fortunately, many other leaders and Imams of mosques had a much better vision of what was needed.

I realized that we needed a way of training young Muslim leaders in America to understand the unique dynamics of this country and the importance of our presence here. Ideally, our Imams would be American-born Muslims, educated in the States, and aware of the issues we face, first hand. An organization that I was involved in, Hartford Seminary, was addressing exactly that through their chaplaincy and Imam training programs, which I will illustrate further on in this book.

After 9/11 many of us began to juggle our priorities. In the day we worked in our professional jobs but after hours we now tried to make ourselves available to answer the questions that our neighbors needed answered. We began to speak in places of worship more frequently, doing radio and television interviews. Local newspapers interviewed us frequently.

But, however hard we tried, there always seemed a louder voice spreading fear of us somewhere. What non-Muslims heard from those voices naturally confused them. Verses of the Qur'an were mistranslated or quoted incompletely and published without context or explanation and those got much more coverage than the true explanations from us American Muslims. The only reason we were losing the battle seemed to be that their message was more 'sensational' and therefore 'newsworthy', as they concocted a scary and violent faith with no resemblance to Islam.

Meanwhile, a similar vilification process of the United States was happening in the rest of the world, especially in the Muslim world, where Americans were being defined with similar broad stereotypes. As extremists in America vilified Muslims, extremists in some Muslim countries began to vilify Jews and Christians where they were minorities. A kind of tit-for-tat disrespect for each other grows from such freely expressed intolerance and contempt, all under the guise of freedom of speech. There is a resultant global village of disrespect for minorities which we can least afford.

An example of this is the cartoons depicting Prophet Muhammad as a terrorist that made some laugh but also brought deep hurt to those who revered the Prophet. Did the person who drew that cartoon feel that hurt or was it only the mocking laughter he or she heard?

We now had to learn not to allow ourselves to be baited. Instead, we had to become mature enough to set the agenda we wanted and to be examples of what we were saying we were, no matter what the provocation was. It is easy to be reactionary but it is also self-destructive. Our role should be to be wise and educated in our response, which is the call to action the Qur'an lays out for us. All adherents of our faith love the Prophet and showing anger against others, even if they insult him, would be an insult to his teachings. Anger solves nothing.

We are taught in kindergarten not to be hurtful and insulting to each other and some adults seem to forget that lesson as they grow older. Yes we respect the U.S. Constitution and Amendments and understand that freedom of speech is a basic and fundamental right, but we know that it was meant to be a tool used against injustice and for the freedom to petition government, not a freedom designed to insult each other.

Chapter 7

Abandoning the Constitution

As fear of Islam spread, due to what was propagated by hate groups, the actions of law enforcement agencies was of real concern. Soon after 9/11 there was a dragnet of arrests, particularly in New York City. Under the guise of national security lots of immigrants, mostly Muslim, were taken into custody. They vanished for months without notification of family or friends. Muslim detainees of that time claim to have been held in solitary confinement and physically abused, simply for being Muslim, while the government fought to prevent judicial oversight of the legality of this outrageous behavior.

And this was in the United States of America where we are supposed to be innocent until proven guilty and have the right to legal counsel! In fact this land was the bastion of civil rights for the whole world and the United States often spoke authoritatively about minority rights through its embassies throughout the world. How could we be circumventing judicial oversight of what we do?

Such 'illegal' law enforcement behavior got even worse! Many detainees were sent back to their home countries for immigration violations. What was troubling was that all this was done in secrecy for 'national security reasons', which gave the impression that the detainees were terrorists, when none of them were. They were instead guilty of immigration violations. There are thousands of immigration violators in the United States and Muslims are a very small portion of this pie. Yet only the Muslims were targeted.

Common Dreams, an on-line news magazine has highlighted some of these issues, which have come up in a class action lawsuit in which 1,200 Muslims and South Asians filed against the U.S. government for unlawful imprisonment and abuse in the aftermath of 9/11[7]. As Bill Goodman from the Center for Constitutional law has said, over 2000 Muslim men were detained, some for many months, and not one of them was found to have any association with terrorism.

We must ask ourselves whether we as a nation over-reacted and made things worse by creating an atmosphere of fear. I think we did, and had to give up some of our cherished values, such as our internationally recognized status in adhering to laws and the upholding of justice.

Many non-Muslim Americans who heard about the large-scale detention policy started believing that if so many Muslims were being arrested and deported, to prevent terrorism, the problem must be real. So the misperception of the war against Islam set in. The Obama administration has done no better than its predecessors in this regard and because of all this nations spying, we are

---

[7] http://www.commondreams.org/headlines06/0125-04.htm

becoming an increasingly feared and hated super-power. This culture of impunity, in my opinion, has directly led to the Julian Assange and Edward Snowden whistle-blower issues.

Another very troubling development, in September 2002, was the Department of Homeland Security's requirement for men from Muslim majority countries 'and North Korea' to register with the Immigration and Nationalization Service, INS. Called 'special registration', it targeted mostly Muslims directly in what was another religiously discriminatory practice.

There were 25 countries in all targeted. Of about 82,500 people who complied, over 13,000 were put into deportation proceedings. As you can imagine, Muslims felt under siege. It was leading to an erosion of our civil rights.

An article by Abdul Malik Mujahid summarized that insecurity we felt in 2003[8]. According to his article; through the dragnet of arrests after 9/11, the FBI had interviewed 27,000 people, 6,483 were detained and 3,208 were deported. Through the special registration process, the FBI had interviewed 144,513 people and 13,434 were in the process of deportation. He felt that the real figures were about double that.

Almost every one of us knew several people who had been interviewed, arrested, or been affected by a raid. These were scary and insecure times and the fact that it was being done by those supposed to protect us made it scarier.

---

[8] http://soundvision.com/info/muslims/internment.asp

According to the National Lawyers Guild, "People with serious breaches of the law are not looked at, while in the Muslim or Arab community somebody with a minor violation automatically gets deported."

The "War on Terror" and the invasion of Afghanistan and then Iraq, increased the fear even more. The color codes used to designate the nation's threat level made people even more fearful that an attack was imminent and they looked to their Muslim neighbors even more suspiciously.

As these invasions were against Muslim majority countries the war rhetoric to rally the forces against the enemy spread into rhetoric against Islam and Muslims in the United States. The Bush administration, especially Vice-President Dick Cheney, Attorney General John Ashcroft, and Defense Secretary Donald Rumsfeld are guilty of using some of the worst rhetoric to spread fear in rallying the nation to accept war.

President Bush's administration introduced words such as Jihadist, Islamist and Islamic-terrorist without apparent concern as to how alienating this language is to American Muslims. Jihad is an Arabic word meaning 'to struggle – for the best' and is usually used to mean a struggle against injustice, it does not mean terror. If you give the terrorist the cover of fighting injustice, then you are encouraging others to join that fight. It was counterproductive in the extreme.

Using Islamic terms was exactly what the terrorists also wanted and that is what the administration unwittingly did, making this war seem more and more like a war against Islam and so, I am sure, this did not hurt their recruiting efforts.

As the war casualties increased there were increased attacks on mosques in the U.S., Muslim women had a harder time because of the way they dressed, and the work place became a more hostile environment for them. Bullying of our children at schools increased and there were difficulties in opening new mosques for prayer throughout the nation. The war rhetoric and insinuations of collusion with the enemy were also getting uglier.

Many people outside of this country who were not Muslim became reluctant to come here. My very close friend, Prashanth, from my medical school in Sri Lanka, who had been so excited that I was coming to America, but did not have the financial means at that time to consider applying, was one of them.

In 2003 there was a need for young medical doctors in the United States, so I contacted him and told him that there was a good chance that he could come and start his medical residency training and the opportunity then to practice in America. Prashanth replied saying, "Reza you must be crazy. I don't know how you can stay on there with the draconian laws that the United States is passing against basic freedoms and the stereotyping of Muslims and Asians. What good is America without the attractions of freedom and opportunity that we all dreamed of? I am now in Australia and would not even consider America...because we have heard of so many instances of even non-Muslim Asians being victimized."

How different it had been when we had rejoiced together at my getting the chance to come to America for my studies. America had lost a ton of credibility in a few years. To many professional men and women abroad the U.S.A was off their list.

Despite all the reassurances, this War on Terror was taking ominous turns. Many Muslim charities were closed, even though they had no connection with 9/11. These charities had been helping Palestinians in the occupied territories and the Palestinian Diaspora throughout the Middle East who were living in refugee camps.

This was a problem, as Muslims have to give 2.5% of our wealth to the poor (poor due or 'Zakat'). It is a central tenet of our faith to do so. Now we could not give in charity to our own organizations, as doing so would put us under suspicion of being accomplices to terror.

Worst of all was the USA PATRIOT Act (United in Strengthening America (by) Providing Appropriate Tools Required to Intercept and Obstruct Terrorism). It was signed into law by President Bush on October 26th 2001. It was a voluminous law that allowed the intelligence community to spy on anybody without a warrant, merely based on suspicion. Needless to say there was huge abuse potential in it. It dramatically reduced restrictions on law enforcement agencies gathering intelligence, broadened the authorities' right to detain and deport immigrants suspected of terrorism, and allowed for wiretapping of oral and electronic communications related to terrorism.

We have on many occasions invited law enforcement, including Federal Bureau of Intelligence (FBI) agents to discussions at our mosques, trying to help as much as we can in this quest to rid this nation of terrorism. They had special outreach agents and we invited one of them, Mr. Ronald Offut, to speak to the leadership of the Muslim community. We asked him directly whether it was true that our phone lines were being tapped and our e-mails intercepted without warrants. His answer was that if the FBI had the tools to fight terrorism they would use them, and more than likely are using those means. He added that this was a political issue and we needed to address it through our elected officials as they had passed the laws giving the FBI those tools.

Although some people said these were freedoms that we could not afford in times of war and we all have to sacrifice for them, it was not 'we all' that were sacrificing, it was *Muslims* who were sacrificing, plain and simple.

Each personally restrictive law passed at this time was being applied to Muslims almost exclusively. I would submit to you that we were thus experiencing a total failure of law enforcement to keep its promise not to religiously profile any community. Representative Peter King and others in government, through the fear they perpetuated, allowed us to be profiled, spied on, and vilified and at the same time they accused us of not helping law enforcement. Building trust entails showing mutual benefit for all and the actions of law enforcement were failing at that.

A major concern that we had was that the negative sentiment and ignorance of Islam had even spread to those entrusted to protecting us. We were especially concerned about the instructions law enforcement and intelligence were getting during their training. There were fear mongers that had infiltrated the training process of local and federal training of our soldiers and other law enforcement and intelligence personnel such as the FBI, the CIA, NYPD and other local and federal law enforcement bodies, as experts. They ratcheted up the fear and hatred against ordinary Muslims. A report in *The New York Times* shows that some of the training material specifically had slides saying "The United States is at war with Islam, and we ought to recognize that we are at war"[9]. I don't think it is fair to only blame the soldiers who go on rampages killing people in Afghanistan without also holding accountable the trainers who trained them in hate. This includes the speakers that are paid by law enforcement and are listed further on.

The *Associated Press (A.P.)* uncovered the effect of this biased training when they reported on the spying of the American Muslim community that was carried out by the New York Police Department without any suspicious activity. This was related in an article in the *Huffington Post,* which showed the degree to which the anti-Muslim rhetoric was now being accepted by law enforcement leadership to go after innocent Muslims through expeditions of surveillance and spying[10].

---

[9] http://www.nytimes.com/2012/04/26/us/new-review-ordered-on-anti-islamic-themes-in-military-courses.html
[10] http://www.huffingtonpost.com/2012/02/21/nypd-spied-on-muslim-stud_n_1290544.html

The A.P. report from 2012 describes the heavy financial resources (tax payers money) used to spy on the Muslim community. Money was even spent monitoring Muslim youth from universities who went on whitewater rafting trips, though other students were not monitored! This, while the intelligence community said to us that they only spy when there is a credible lead. In this case there was none and the Police Chief who followed Ray Kelly, Bill Bratton, abandoned that spy program saying it had produced no worthwhile information[11].

In the theatre of war the training deficit had more dire consequences, as happened in the case of Calvin Gibbs, who killed innocent civilians as a sport, as reported in the *New York Times* in 2011[12]. Soldiers urinated on dead Afghans, disrespected the Qur'an, and tortured and abused prisoners in places like Abu Ghraib. In this digitally connected age, pictures of all of these went viral, in particular in the Muslim world. Does this not create more hatred and anger and help entice more people to join the other side?

I learned in my medical training that if you want to understand a problem you have to look at the whole disease process not just the symptoms that are visible from the outside. If we antagonize people in other countries and our own and disrespect their faith and the followers of their faith then it plays into the hands of the terrorists. They use this as a recruiting tool by propagating the notion that we, in the U.S., are at war with Islam.

---

[11] http://www.nytimes.com/2014/04/16/nyregion/police-unit-that-spied-on-muslims-is-disbanded.html?_r=0
[12] http://www.nytimes.com/2011/11/11/us/calvin-gibbs-convicted-of-killing-civilians-in-afghanistan.html?

Thus they cause even more death and destruction and attract more followers.

Back at home, the Muslim community has in fact been most helpful in preventing domestic terror acts by their vigilance working together with law enforcement. We have been helping law enforcement by constantly telling our communities to be aware of anything unusual and speak up if they are concerned. This should be acknowledged, publicized and the Muslim community encouraged much more.

For example the person who first tipped off law enforcement about the Time square bomb that failed to go off, in downtown Manhattan was a Muslim. The *American Muslim journal* has written about the many times that the American Muslim community has been instrumental in thwarting domestic terrorist attacks by tipping off law enforcement[13]. According to that article Muslim communities have helped law enforcement prevent nearly two-thirds of all Al-Qaeda related plots threatening the U.S. since December 2009.

Our standing, as a bastion of human rights and a light to the world has been most affected through 'black prisons', where we outsourced "advanced interrogation techniques" (read as torture), to other nations. Abu Ghraib, the Iraqi prison infamous for the prisoner abuse that took place there, is just a symptom of the erosion of human rights and our values through our acceptance of advanced interrogation techniques:

---

[13] http://theamericanmuslim.org/tam.php/features/articles/american-muslims-cooperation-with-law-enforcement

From late 2003 to early 2004, during the Iraq War, military police personnel of the United States Army and the Central Intelligence Agency committed human rights violations against prisoners held in the Abu Ghraib prison. They physically and sexually abused, tortured, raped, sodomized, and killed prisoners, outsourcing and legalizing torture and allowing water boarding as permissible, despite worldwide condemnation of it.

Wikipedia

Domestically things were also getting worse. Craig Monteilh reported, in April 2012, on what the FBI was having informants do, in an article in *Russia Today*[14]. Monteilh spied on the Muslim community in California for several years. The FBI gave him key-tag recording devices that he left around mosques, and in Imam's offices, cars and homes. But he began to reflect on what was being done and decided it was unjust. He felt the war on terror was becoming a religious war on Islam and so he went public with his story. He said that the FBI blackmailed individuals by threatening to expose any information they could uncover, such as extramarital affairs or immigration violations, to force them to become informants. Everything he did was protected under national security.

A book called *'The Terror Factory: Inside the FBI's Manufactured War on Terrorism'* by Trevor Aaronson, a California based investigative journalist, reveals even more of what has been done against the Muslim community.

---

[14] http://www.youtube.com/watch?v=7DlSAwkh1C8

It is difficult to imagine this new United States. The loss in this nation of legal norms and due process with impartiality that we all grew up with has been shocking. True patriotism should be about pointing this out and not blindly giving in to self-defeating actions.

Benjamin Franklin said, "Those who would give up essential liberty to purchase a little temporary safety deserve neither liberty nor security." How we yearn for a leader these days with the wisdom and vision of Benjamin Franklin. What happened to "Give me liberty or give me death" by Patrick Henry, one of our Founding Fathers? We have to go back to being who we were and, deep inside still are. I adore the United States I came to, but with all the spying and political scapegoating that United States has changed a lot.

Have the terrorists in fact achieved their objectives if they have changed that free spirit of America so much?

I am writing to ask you to join with me to prevent that from happening any more. We must not give in to fears and allow others to destroy the country we love and the values we all cherish.

Chapter 8

The Tail That Wags the Dog

Thankfully, in the United States, because of the system of checks and balances, 'we the people' have the tools to fight against government and intelligence overstepping their bounds.

The American Civil Liberties Union and the Council of American Islamic Relations have kept the Muslim community aware of the abuses of the law and also of our rights, which include the right to a lawyer prior to speaking to intelligence agents.

We often get the question "If you have nothing to fear why would you need a lawyer when Intelligence agents question you?" The answer is that in our experience some agents go beyond the law when they question Muslims. Whether they do it because they are overzealous, under direction from superiors, or for other reasons is not known, but they do it and they blackmail some people they question. Muslims have informed us that agents have tried to recruit them as informants offering as a reward that their immigration violations would be overlooked if they just spied on their mosque communities.

When we bring up these facts with other FBI agents that are meant to reach out to us the reply we get is that these are simply overzealous intelligence officers. It is happening a little too frequently to be isolated cases.

I have often wondered what exactly so-called 'over-zealous' agents are looking for. We have been told they want names of people who frequent mosques. But those who frequent mosques are the most spiritually secure, not the ones likely to cause terror and kill and maim, as those actions are far from what the religion of Islam teaches or allows. We often tried to tell this to our intelligence agents but it didn't seem to stop them from focusing on the mosques. It seemed like someone else was telling them to keep spying on the mosques. We kept telling them to focus instead on the dejected and isolated loners who are at much more risk for carrying out acts of reprisal.

Take the case of Faisal Shahzad, the man who attempted to set off the bomb in Times Square. As Faisal Shahzad was from Connecticut, where I live, we investigated and realized that he was not someone who frequented a mosque and in fact *was* a loner. He had got disgruntled with the wars in his homeland, Pakistan, where the drone attacks were killing innocent civilians and therefore decided to take the law into his own hands and try to avenge these killings.

Our concern was that law enforcement officers were led to believe, through agenda-driven training, that the terror-prone people are those regular Muslims who frequent mosques, and that is where counter-terrorism training failed. That kind of thinking makes law enforcement and our intelligence community focus in the wrong direction and, in doing so, lose a natural ally in the mosque community and its leadership, people who are available and eager to help. The NYPD spying case highlighted this misguided intelligence focus.

We also missed the opportunity, at that early stage, to see what was out there on the internet and social media that was really radicalizing our youth. If at that time our intelligence agents had listened to us and had focused on the loners and not gotten distracted into spying on mosques, we would be vastly better off today as we realize that ISIS and other terror groups troll the internet for vulnerable and isolated Muslims to prey on.

On February 3rd 2012, a CNN story from Iowa illustrated this counter-productive phenomenon. In 2002, Arvinder Singh, a Sikh, was asked to spy on the Muslim community and took on the name 'Rafik Alvi'. He was asked to infiltrate the community and sometimes wired when going to the mosque. Though he was a Sikh he was required to pretend to be a Muslim while conducting his subversive activities. At this time the FBI was stating that it only uses the 'PATRIOT Act' when there had already been a credible threat of terrorism, which was clearly untrue in this case.

Singh spied on at least four mosques for the FBI because he was promised that he would be made a US citizen if he did. He says that the FBI recanted on this and, therefore, he spilled the beans feeling unrewarded and betrayed by the FBI.

Could a Christian or a Jew or a person of any other faith feel secure if he was unsure who could be trusted in his place of worship? A mosque should be a place for prayer, for reflection and serenity as are churches, synagogues, and temples. You go there to seek spiritual solace and a deepening connection with your Creator. You go also to experience the fellowship of other believers. The suspicion that members of the community may in fact be FBI spies only pretending to be of our religion has led to a breakdown of trust, both between law enforcement and the Muslim community, and within the Muslim community itself. Somehow these stories keep getting reported on but nothing seems to stop the abuses.

This country witnessed similar scapegoating when our enemy was the Soviet Union. In the 1950's, Senator McCarthy famously made claims that Communists and Soviet spies had infiltrated the US Government. His claims were unsubstantiated and he was eventually censured by the Senate. Today McCarthyism is used to refer to bigoted and unsubstantiated accusations and public attacks on the patriotism of a group or religious or ethnic minority.

When McCarthyism was at its peak, a long list of U.S. citizens suddenly became unemployable, though they had done nothing against their country. Employers worried that if they employed the men and women McCarthy listed they themselves would be accused of being underground spies for the Soviet Union.

The Muslim leadership who had been working with the FBI, naturally felt betrayed by what the intelligence community was doing. Embedded informants used in human fishing expeditions do not build trust or confidence. Once trust has been lost it is difficult to trust fully again.

The intelligence community must realize that alienating the Muslim community is counter-productive in achieving the goals of ridding this nation of terrorism. Making our citizens lose confidence in law enforcement is a result that none of us or our country can afford. Where is all this suspicion and paranoia on the part of intelligence coming from? Once again, I believe it comes down to their tainted training.

We know now that law enforcement actually went further than spying on us in the Muslim community. Law enforcement gave some people in the community the idea of blowing up buildings and promised them support if they did and then arrested them with lots of publicity when they took the idea seriously. These agents were called 'Agent provocateurs' and such 'entrapment' has been used by law enforcement frequently.

Craig Monteilh, the FBI informant who had a change of heart, says he was paid a lot of money for what he did but believed later was immoral. He felt that such techniques were a grave injustice as those people would not have done what they were being coerced to do without 'assistance'.

The FBI created many of the "terrorist plots" foiled by law enforcement (*Russia Today*). Such entrapment happened in the case of the 'Newburgh Four'. An agent provocateur named Hussain offered financial inducements, including $250,000 to one man, to carry out and place bombs in Jewish synagogues and businesses.

The jobs were offered to poor black Muslims in the economically deprived city of Newburgh in New York who could be easily tempted by money. When they were arrested, with great media attention, the whole Muslim community was in the spotlight as being anti-Semitic, though these were all intelligence driven operations.

The Guardian newspaper in a December 2010 article said, "It raises serious questions about how the FBI is treating the Muslim communities in America."[15]

Is our country making headway against terrorists or just trying to justify the enormous cost of law enforcement in this post 9/11 era? This was almost ten years after the terror attacks. Aren't we destroying the delicate fabric of tolerance and respect for each other this nation was founded on? Aren't we also causing a lot of collateral damage to our image throughout the world?

According to Russia Today Somali-born Mohamed Osman Mohamud the 'Christmas tree bomber' was aided and abetted, that is, their crimes were 'assisted' by entrapment[16]. He was tempted by this sting into attempting to blow up the Portland annual Christmas lighting celebration in November 2010 and then arrested with lots of publicity as a victory for law enforcement.

The cost of this counter-terrorism is 3.3 billion dollars of the FBI budget. Mother Jones, a news magazine that does investigative reporting, says there are 15,000 spies, most tasked with infiltrating the Muslim community[17]. Yet between 1956 and 1971, with

[15] http://www.guardian.co.uk/world/2011/dec/12/newburgh-four-fbi-entrapment-terror
[16] http://www.youtube.com/watch?v=YIx4ZDR3fv8
[17] http://www.motherjones.com/politics/2011/08/fbi-terrorist-informants

COINTELPRO (Counter Intelligence Program), the FBI had only 1,500 spies using techniques, including character assassinations, harassment, and illegal violence including actual assassinations against the then enemy, the Communists.

COINTELPRO was a series of covert and at times illegal projects conducted by the United States Federal Bureau of Investigation aimed at surveying, infiltrating, discrediting and disrupting domestic political organizations. When COINTELPRO was exposed after a burglary it was promptly abandoned.

We have ten times the number of spies now tasked with targeting the Muslim community. Is it unnatural to feel concerned?

According to *Mother Jones,* of the 508 terrorist cases they investigated, nearly half of the cases involved informants, and led to 158 prosecutions. Of these 158, 49 were led by agent provocateurs that, as in the case of the Newburgh four in December 2011, may have been caused by paying people to commit crimes.

There is a vicious cycle at play here: the more "terrorists" are caught, the more people get scared, more laws are then passed restricting our freedoms, and more money is allocated for this type of law enforcement. *Mother Jones* reports that all but 3 of the high profile domestic terror plots were FBI stings. It is no wonder, then, that in December 2011, more than ten years after the terror attacks of 9/11, the PATRIOT Act was not only passed, it was reinforced and expanded by the NDAA (National Defense Appropriations Act), which allows for American citizens to be held indefinitely without due process.

The tail is wagging the dog to extreme dizziness and economic and financial meltdown. We are destroying ourselves from within and if we continue this irrational fear, it will consume us.

Chapter 9

Spreading Fear

As Muslims we needed some benchmarks to see how we were doing in terms of clarifying to our neighbors who we are. I was shocked to learn that after the *Time* magazine poll of 2001, subsequent polls in fact showed that the number of those that had a negative impression of us kept rising with time, despite everything we were doing to be better understood. In 2005 a Pew Research center poll found that our 'unfavorability' rating went up to a shocking 36% - more than twice the Time Magazine 2001 figure, which was 17%. An increase from 17% to 36% is the equivalent of 60 million more people[18]. I now had to face the fact that 60 million more people or 115 million people in total, in my chosen country, had an unfavorable view of people of my faith.

In August 2010 we were being seen 'unfavorably' by between 38 and 45% of all Americans. We thought to ourselves it can't get any worse but in 2015 that number was more than 50%. About 160 million people had an unfavorable view of us.

---

[18] http://www.people-press.org/2010/08/24/public-remains-conflicted-over-islam/

It was mind-boggling. It was frightening. Can there be a healthy relationship between the majority of Muslims, who want to contribute to this nation's success, while being viewed negatively by more than half the population? Some of us are strong enough to know that we have to change this narrative but what about our youth who have to deal with the negative perceptions about their religion on television, social media and perhaps even from bullies in their schools? We have to address these issues if we are to get beyond the fear to the process of healing and preventing these same youth from becoming fodder for ISIS propaganda on social media.

My job, once again, as a physician is to analyze a problem, usually a disease process, and come up with a solution or a treatment plan. I set about studying our 'un-favorability' the same way. Analyzing the problem and then finding a way we could turn things around. In this book I will take you through that process of analyzing the challenges we faced and how we dealt with them in our state and the greater Hartford area in particular.

Here is a major problem: in a major study by the Center for American Progress termed 'Fear Inc.', the authors describe a hate industry, Islamophobia, directed by a few individuals, some of whom I will describe further on, that had earned $42.6 million dollars up to 2011, polluting media analyses, affecting law enforcement training, and influencing politicians with their hatred[19]. This answered a lot of questions about the fear and hate that was being spread. Nathan Lean wrote the book "The

---

[19] http://www.americanprogress.org/issues/2011/08/islamophobia.html

Islamophobia Industry" which gives a historical perspective on the racism and xenophobia of the individuals of this industry and the Media's involvement as well as the blogospheres contribution to this.

For example, the Norwegian self-proclaimed terrorist, Anders Breivik, killed eight people when he detonated a van-bomb in Oslo and then went to a summer camp for the Workers Youth League and killed 69 people there, killing a total of 77 and injuring 319 more. He quotes many American Islamophobes, those irrational haters of Islam, in his manifesto to justify his murderous actions. He killed them because he felt they were supportive of integration. It seems there were no consequences for spreading hate about Islam, even if it led to murder and terrorism.

I realized we had to wake up and accept that we could not, as a nation, afford to have such hate mongers direct and control the way we all live.

The influence scare mongers have on politicians, who often only focus on their re-election campaign, is also a huge problem. As a result of the fear some politicians have highlighted 'shariah law' or some other Arabic term as a rallying call on which to base their campaign 'pseudo' strength in national security terms. This was highlighted in the presidential debates of the Republican Party in 2012, when every candidate said they would ban 'shariah law' (the guidelines that Muslims use to live a morally and spiritually fulfilling life), and none of them knew what shariah was, they had just been fed by extremists on their biased perceptions of it. Before 'shariah law' it was 'jihad' (a struggle against oppression). Arabic terms, that were never defined correctly, were used to scare people into fearing Islam.

In this election cycle Ted Cruz and Donald Trump have made it their campaign mission to call out President Obama for not calling the terrorists "radical Islamic terrorists" or "Jihadists", trying to unfairly connect the religion to these terrorists. This is the textbook definition of demagoguery, a political leader who gains power by arousing people's emotions and prejudices. Cruz scares me more than Trump does in this regard as he has been fixated on painting Islam negatively his whole political life. He is also a good orator, which is a trademark of many a demagogue.

Those obsessed with trying to keep hate afloat are so effective that ten years after the 9/11 terror attacks this country was still ratcheting up laws that should have been relaxed so that people could get on with their lives. The National Defense Authorization Act, passed at the end of December of 2011, however, went even further in giving law enforcement and intelligence even broader powers; powers to arrest American citizens on suspicion of terrorist-related activities without due process. This sends chills down our collective spines. Is this the America of 'innocent until proven guilty'?

I have found that many of our elected officials don't bother to investigate the truth but just go with popular misconceptions when it comes to Islam - that's what wins votes. We expected President Obama to reassure the people and encourage them to get on with their lives and no longer live in suspicion and fear of their neighbors. We expected him to start winding down these intrusive laws. The opposite has happened. It is as if politicians are increasing the laws and the monitoring of Muslims to appease those who spread fear and hate, both locally and nationally. It is a vicious cycle and we need politicians who are sincere and truly concerned about the situation to reach out to American Muslims who are the most victimized in this non-ending hate. We need politicians to be honest with themselves and begin a process of dialogue and reconciliation – enough fear, enough hate.

Our hopes that President Obama would bring much needed 'Hope' and 'Change' in particular with regard to this never ending "war on terror" have been bargained away by the President, to buy compromise currency. What I mean by this is that he has had to water down his principled stand on various issues due to pressure to have Congress agree with him on other issues, weakening his moral and ethical stand on many issues. He said so much when signing the NDAA Act of 2011, promising that he would never use it himself in arresting American citizens without due process. If it is so repugnant to him I wonder why he would allow it for others who follow him.

On Sundays I teach high school students in the mosque. It is their last year before College and so I challenge them to address issues pertaining to the practical aspects of what they have learned over all these years and how it can be applied in America now. I enjoy the dialogue but during the discourse many of them do admit that they often had to face subtle bullying and taunting because of the portrayal of their religion in the media. They often feel torn between their religion and dealing with what has become a Cold-War against it. Some Muslim youth feel embarrassed to say they are Muslims at school. I am optimistic, however, as a recent Pew Research study has found that it is the younger generation of non-Muslims who are least likely to blindly accept the hate of others. That's good news.

We have to proactively reach out and we began in Connecticut by getting to know our neighbors and them us, through interaction and outreach. I explain this organized approach to outreach in chapters 12 to 15 of this book. We found new friends who began to understand that like them, we or our forebears had come to the United States for "freedom, political liberty, religious freedom, economic opportunity and to practice our religion and escape persecution". This phrase comes directly from the book teaching new citizens why people came to this nation and that has not changed in over 200 years.

In most cases, after the opportunity we had to explain our faith at places of worship, education and many other settings people formed lines to tell us that their impression of Islam and Muslims was based on false information transmitted to them by the media. Now, since they had met a Muslim, that impression had changed. I called these opportunities to meet our neighbors and break bread together - 'Open Houses'. They expressed how they now realized how much we all have in common and how our religion had been distorted to them. They were grateful that we had shown the courage to educate them on the truth of Islam.

Every time we get together now to discuss the predicament of the world we live in, we realize that the enemy is within each of our faiths – as the extremists practice it. Together we must honestly consider and offer tangible solutions to the problems that we face.

This extremist minority, that distorts each other's faiths is present in all our faiths and has the mentality of 'live and let die'. This is very different from the teachings of the messengers who brought revelation to us, including Moses, Jesus and Muhammad. All you have to do is read their teachings, including the Qur'an, to see this. This, however, must be done through understanding a faith through an adherent of that faith and not reading the cherry picked verses extremists would like you to read, out of context.

Chapter 10

Delegitimized and Stigmatized.

I was at a recent 'Open House' event at a mosque and a Catholic attendee, during the Q and A session asked "I really want to hear the mainstream voice of Islam and cannot find it. I looked up the Islamic Society of North America, as it seemed a legitimate voice of Muslims, and found that even they had a terrorist connection as they were classified as 'unindicted co-conspirators'. Who do we go to when we want to know about Islam?"

This is a sore area for the Muslim community as our national organizations are kept under a cloud of suspicion due to this designation of 'unindicted co-conspirators'. It means they have not been indicted for anything criminal but are in this limbo area of suspicion of working with someone else that is also under suspicion. It is very confusing and directly affects the authority of leadership in the Muslim community.

The Islamic Society of North America (ISNA) is the largest Muslim organization in North America. Tens of thousands of Muslims attend its annual conference, but it is classified by the Federal government as an unindicted co-conspirator and has been so for over a decade. Although there have been wild accusations of having historical connections with the Egyptian group called the 'Muslim Brotherhood', it has never been found to have a direct connection with terrorism. Its taxes were examined by the Senate Finance committee in 2003, and it was given a clean bill, but the name 'unindicted co-conspirators' has not been withdrawn by the Federal Government. This keeps the Muslim leadership in suspicion of being connected to the type of terrorists who claimed ownership of 9/11.

Any leader who takes a role in these organizations is automatically under scrutiny, considered a suspect and so accused of a criminal connection when invited to speak. Obviously, this 'guilt by association' limits who will take these positions of leadership. The burden of having to prove that you are innocent of something you are incapable of challenging is surely not what is expected of 'a free society' and the adage 'innocent until proven guilty'. Fortunately, leaders of other religious communities come to ISNA conferences risking the accusation that they are thus associating with an unindicted co-conspirator.

A good friend of my family, Dr. Ingrid Mattson, the former President of ISNA and a professor of Islam & Christian Muslim Relations at Hartford Seminary here in Connecticut, should have been embraced by the American media and law enforcement for her accomplishments. Dr. Mattson is a Canadian-born convert to Islam and a scholar of Islamic law. She is a woman who was elected to lead the largest Muslim organization in the nation. What better role model can you want as a Muslim leader with all the accusations about the treatment of women in Islam?

During her tenure as President of ISNA, she had audiences with two presidents (Bush and Obama) and was invited to the White House on numerous occasions by both presidents. Despite that, she has to deal with the fact that she is the head of an organization still referred to as an 'unindicted co-conspirator', a label she does not deserve. She is an eloquent speaker, often called to speak about the need to work together, but at these speaking engagements she would often have to face questions about her status as head of an organization that is an unindicted co-conspirator. There were the questioners that were there to smear the Muslim leadership and so would often throw this accusation at her in public.

Likewise, the Council on American Islamic Relations, CAIR, is a civil rights organization, just like the American Civil Liberties Union (ACLU) and the Anti-Defamation League (ADL), which was also labeled as an unindicted co-conspirator because of similar historical connections with a charity that helps Palestinian refugees. In spite of its good work CAIR has its hecklers too, and its members feel as if there is a shadow surrounding all that they do.

As CAIR is a civil rights organization and Muslims are going through some of the toughest civil rights challenges of any community, Muslims still go to them to seek their advice, but risk being targeted negatively simply for seeking their help. What with spying, entrapment and agent provocateurs, we need a robust civil rights organization to explain to our community the challenges we face and the rights we have. Unfortunately, many Muslims are scared to go to them because of the 'unindicted co-conspirator' label. It is not healthy for a community to feel under siege and have no recourse to help itself.

We are very concerned that with so much stacked up against our community our youth would be affected negatively. We wanted them to feel proud of both their U.S. identity and their Islamic identity and heritage. We certainly did not feel that there was anything incompatible with these two identities.

We wanted our youth to come to our mosques, just as other religions provide a place of spiritual guidance for their youth. We did not want young Muslims to feel isolated, because that makes them unpredictable. In the mosques we preach that our religion has nothing to do with the war against terrorism and we give them a positive identity as American Muslims, which is in fact the same message our government proclaims.

I believe the Muslim leadership throughout the country deserves a lot of credit for keeping hope alive, especially among the youth, but for how long can we do this without assistance? My understanding of Islam has enabled me to respond with patience and steadfastness, rather than with anger or despondence.

As their 'Sunday Islamic school' teacher, I realized many high school teens were going through identity crises. They wanted to be proud of their faith and their nationality but felt there was a 'clash' between the two and that somehow they had to choose between one and the other. When I dug a little deeper, their insecurity was always based on the media's portrayal of Islam. Only in the safety of the mosque, surrounded by their Muslim peers could they open up.

A youth in Connecticut, Syed Mansoor Alam, has written a book about his experience which he called 'Ten Years Older' (published in 2011).

In 'Ten Years Older', Mansoor describes his initial thoughts (he was only 8 years old) after the September 11th attacks. "I felt Islam had betrayed me. I didn't want to be identified as a Muslim kid."

Nevertheless his peers called him "that Muslim kid".

A friend of his, Ray Noonan confirms that. "There are always comments being made. People make it seem like it's not a big deal, but on the inside it affects young people".

Alam became sick and missed a whole year of schooling, until he finally spoke at a conference on radicalization, and came to the conclusion that in school "Muslims are radicalized by bullying and harassment!"

I don't think it is very different for adults. If you are made to feel isolated and harassed, you may not be the most stable in your identity as an American Muslim who will contribute to our nation's betterment. I wish Rep. Peter King had included Mansoor in his Congressional hearings on radicalization.

The *Record Journal* published a very informative article about him in September 2011[20]. He was a student at Wesleyan University at the time, and he has since started the non-profit organization 'ENOUGH'. He is, despite this challenging past, a very confident young man now.

Some of his experiences correspond very closely to the experiences of the youth I teach. I have, however, found that when our youth are involved and participate in service in soup kitchens and 'Habitat' builds that the Muslim community, through the Muslim Coalition of Connecticut, is involved in, they become strong advocates of positive U.S. and Islamic values. This is exactly what I want to instill in them, so they become self-confident in their identity as American Muslims. These youth are going to embrace U.S. and Islamic values and change things for the better. I am confident of this.

Youth brought up in a nurturing setting in mosques are not going to commit crimes against this or any country. They are going to try and stop crime, like the Muslim Alioune Niasse, the Senegalese immigrant who called a policeman when he noticed smoke coming from an abandoned car, leading to the apprehension of the Times Square bombing suspect.

Sadly, the media shut their eyes to Niasse's contribution and on May 5 *Think Progress* published a headline 'Media Ignore the Fact that Man who Alerted Police to Failed Times Square Bombing

---

[20] http://www.myrecordjournal.com/cheshire/article_b4bddf40-da8d-11e0-877b-001cc4c03286.html

is a Muslim Immigrant.' The media ignored it because it was not 'sensational' or 'newsworthy'.

We are only being known for the negatives, the media does not consider the positive contributions to be newsworthy. This is a recipe for disaster unless we are all, including the media, willing to be more responsible in reporting and highlighting the positives too. If this is not done, the sense of siege in the community will worsen and sadly, through social media, outside forces will continue to worsen the process of 'radicalization' of our youth.

Chapter 11

The President of the United States

The President of the United States and what he says has a big impact on the tempo and climate of the country, especially in difficult times.

President Bush, in the beginning of his term as president, had the good will to differentiate the terrorists from Muslim practitioners and the religion of Islam. However, he was dominated by his Vice President and he did not enforce or establish his leadership over the direction that the vice president decided to take us, at least through the latter's control of events behind the scenes. That I think is why Dick Cheney, as vice president could and did become such a powerful force in the nation. His office played a huge role, we now know, in pushing the war on Iraq, and in influencing then Secretary of State, Colin Powell, to say what he did about weapons of mass destruction at the United Nations.

It was clearly an ideological war forced down the throats of tax payers through a Neocon agenda, driven by a few zealots including Paul Wolfowitz, Richard Perle and Elliott Abrams and completely illegal by international law.

The illegality of some of what went on in the Vice President's office resulted in the indictment and prison sentence, which President Bush commuted, of Scooter Libby, the Vice President's Chief of Staff on charges of perjury, obstruction of justice, and lying to investigators.

Although the Obama presidential campaign of 2008 was a tough time for Muslims, partly due to conspiracy theories of him being a Muslim, after his election, he and his administration were a huge breath of fresh air. He stopped the inappropriate use of Islamic terms when speaking about terrorists, and we could almost see the light we had been looking for at the end of the tunnel. Terms such as 'Jihadist' for terrorist, and Islamist for extremist had been used freely by many of the Bush administration officials, and their alienating effect on the Muslim community was paid attention to now. President Obama reflected a longed for respect for us, as Muslims in America. He even mentioned Muslims as part of the diversity of the United States in his inaugural address.

In Obama's acknowledgement of Muslims as part of the U.S, we felt a sense of belonging and pride that the President should at least mention us. In the atmosphere of that time it was a big deal for us. Obama also followed this with significant actions that meant a whole lot to Muslims. He went to Cairo, the seat of one of the oldest Islamic education institution in the world.

Cairo was amazing! There was the President of the United States with a common Muslim second name, using the common Muslim greeting 'Assalaamu-alaikum' – 'Peace be with you'.

He also analyzed the problems facing Muslims and the United States in very easy to understand terms. He saw that focusing on our differences would only bring more conflict. He acknowledged that Islam as a religion has the same values as the United States: justice, tolerance, and dignity for all. He expressed the need for mutual respect in helping one another find common ground, saying "the interests we share as human beings are far more powerful than the forces that drive us apart." He reminded people that his father was a Muslim and of his years in Indonesia hearing the Islamic 'call to prayer' – the 'azan'. He also said in no uncertain terms that he is a Christian, which Muslims respect and all people should.

Obama also acknowledged civilization's debt to Islam and Muslims for the enlightenment of Europe, the discovery of algebra, the compass, tools of navigation, and many advances in medicine. He highlighted the history of Islamic tolerance and the fostering of racial equality.

He also acknowledged the Muslim contribution to the history of the United States, and pointed out the fact that Morocco was the first country to recognize our country. He reminded people that it was in the Treaty of Tripoli that the second President of the United States, John Adams, wrote that the United States has no enmity towards the laws, religion or tranquility of Muslims. He was literally talking about Shariah guidelines, how enlightened a president John Adams must have been. Obama also listed American Muslim contributions to our country from sports greats like Muhammad Ali to Hakeem Olajuwon.

He talked about Thomas Jefferson's Qur'an. Thomas Jefferson may even have used Qur'anic guidelines in helping craft the Constitution of the United States of America. Some may find this difficult to believe, but for those who know Islamic guidelines, it is not very different from the U.S. Constitution and the rights of the individual (see chapters on Islam at the end). Obama ended by saying that we needed to base our relationship with Muslims on what Islam *IS*, not on what it is not.

For Muslims in the U.S, having this knowledgeable a president, answering the very issues that those who spread fear were attacking us on, was an immense relief. He also said he would fight against negative stereotypes of Islam as his duty as President of the United States. He spoke about what our country was, in the proudest terms, which resonated with the Cairo audience, and he asked Muslims not to stereotype the United States either. He went on to say our challenges are shared as we all realize that there are extremists on all sides. He illustrated the problems we face starting with violent extremism, but acknowledged mistakes made by the United States including the permitting of some forms of torture, which Dick Cheney to this day does not acknowledge.

His second topic was the Israeli/Palestinian conflict. After explaining the U.S.'s unique relationship with Israel and the need to stop denying the holocaust, he said anti-Semitism, which is unfortunately present in some parts of the Muslim and non-Muslim world, must be stamped out. He spoke about the Muslim and Christian Palestinian's right to a homeland and acknowledged the

Palestinian Diaspora and our responsibility to the aspirations of the Palestinians, their dignity, and the right to a home of their own.

Contrast this with Newt Gingrich who, during his failed presidential bid in 2012, declared that Palestinians are an invented people, while pandering to Sheldon Adelson, a particularly wealthy donor, who was spreading more discord in the Middle East by subsidizing illegal settlements in the occupied territories. According to *New York Times* writer Thomas Friedman, Adelson "personifies everything that is poisoning our democracy and Israel's today."

"The present status is intolerable", the President of the United States said to great applause. Muslims in Cairo and throughout the world needed to hear that the president understood the suffering of the Palestinian occupied people, and in this phrase they understood that acknowledgement.

He then mentioned the need for Palestinians to abandon violence, and Israel to give up on illegal settlement building, saying very firmly that the United States does not accept continued Israeli settlements. He acknowledged that the human rights violations in Gaza by Israel do not serve Israel's security and spoke of the need to ease restrictions on Palestinians who are trying simply to live and work.

The third issue he dealt with was Iran, a dynamically changing political challenge, and the fourth issue was democracy, acknowledging that no country should impose democracy on another, thus abandoning the Bush doctrine of imposed democracy, so detested and alien to the Arab streets. Obama acknowledged his commitment to governments that reflect the will of the people and the people's natural yearning for the basic freedoms that democracy, and not dictatorships, allow them. He also mentioned the need for government transparency and that leaders not steal from the people, which everybody knows these Arab dictators and monarchs do. He pressed the need for addressing human rights for the people of the Muslim and Arab world. He addressed freedom of religion, and gave the example of Andalusia, Islamic Spain and its Capital, Cordoba, and Indonesia, his home for a time, where freedom of religion thrives; stressing that it was an Islamic value.

He acknowledged the rights of Muslim women to wear their form of head covering and addressed women's rights in the Muslim world, where in some quarters there is often a prevention of women's education, despite Islam. Restricting education has nothing to do with Islam, as he illustrated by pointing out the fact that there have been several Muslim women heads of state.

The President also said we cannot pretend to hide behind hostility under the guise of liberalism, which most people realize happened in France with the banning of the head scarf in public places, and in Switzerland with the banning of minarets. He spoke about interfaith services that can make religion a tool for service to humanity, and ended by talking about education and commerce and the need to work together to help Muslims. Speaking to the younger people he said, "You have the ability to change the world."

He addressed issues that were sometimes tough for the Muslim world to hear and others, that showed a deep appreciation and understanding of the religion and the cultural diversity of the Muslim world. I believe it gave Muslims all over the world a sense of optimism for the future, it certainly did so for American Muslims. I sincerely believe that he sowed some of the seeds of the Arab uprisings. The Arabs were so fed up with leaders like Mubarak of Egypt and Assad of Syria that it was about time they had the genuine aspirations of their people heard through genuine elections, not the sham elections that the Arab world is so sick of.

President Obama's visit to Turkey, likewise, was welcomed with great celebration by American Muslims, as he was acknowledging our places of worship and governments that chose to value their Islamic heritage and democratic principles. Prime Minister Erdogan of Turkey is deeply respected for successfully navigating Turkey from a military dictatorship into a modern democracy. In the eyes of the majority of Muslims Turkey may be the model that the Arab spring is most inspired by.

Muslims from the Middle East to Africa, where Obama's father was from, to Asia where Obama studied in, all regarded Barack Hussein Obama as their son. We still retain the ability through our actions to win the respect of the people of the Middle East and for harmony in the world, but we have to work on these relationships and not grandstand in arrogance.

This coming presidential election in 2016 could send a positive message of engagement with the world or an arrogant message of isolation, pitting civilizations against each other. The world cannot afford the latter and so I hope we choose the candidate that will bring us closest to the goal of improving our standing in the world. That comes from returning to our Founding Father's vision of a forward looking, self confident nation and the president of the United States retains the ability to project that.

Chapter 12

Open Houses of Worship

When the prophet entered Medina at the age of fifty three, after being expelled from Makkah, in one of his first speeches he proclaimed "Be a people that spread peace, feed others, maintain family relations, keep up part of the night in prayer and I will be with you in heaven". It was a call to become peacemakers starting out with breaking bread together.

Muslims, as his followers, are known for the opposite of this in the United States at the present time, but it does not mean we cannot strive to change that perception. That, in summary, is what the 'open house' concept aims to do.

The concept of the open house, as I define it in this book, is any opportunity for diverse communities in one area to get to know each other better, usually while enjoying a meal together. Open houses give us a chance to learn about one another in a nurturing setting and with mutual respect for everyone around the table.

Our open houses were tailored specifically to counter the alienation and negative portrayal we, as Muslims, suffered after 9/11. We had been getting to know one another before 9/11, but after it, realized the urgent need for a deeper dialogue between Muslims and non-Muslims everywhere. We found there were opportunities anyone could take advantage of to be better understood. I thought it important to explain what we did so that you too can be a part of this process.

The spirit and idea of the open house, from an Islamic perspective, comes directly from the command of God in the Qur'an:

"O mankind, we created you from a single male and female and divided you into nations and tribes so that you may get to know each other. Verily the most honored of you in the sight of God is the most righteous among you"

(Qur'an 49:13).

Our first step was to reach out to community members and leaders who were brought up in different faiths from ours and the first lesson we learned was that our neighbors warmed towards us for doing so.

Diversity is our biggest strength in the United States, and division through fear and mistrust, our biggest enemy. This country has had a history of understanding this dynamic, and has welcomed people from all faith communities and races to our shores. Immigrants created the United States and our Founding

Fathers wrote the Constitution and Amendments with our diversity in mind. That diversity, however, has also given us a history of initial mistrust of new immigrant groups resulting, sometimes, in a not-so-hearty welcome of them. I refer to the initial waves of Irish Catholics, Italian and Jewish migration to this country.

I believe this mistrust occurs despite our Constitutional and national laws, and is due more to the insecurities that we all have deep inside us, than a natural hostility to people we don't know. The Irish Catholics, the Italians and the Jews all tell us how tough their initial transition was.

So we had to decide how, as Muslims who wanted to be involved in the healing of our nations emotional wounds, we could make our acquaintances into our friends. In 2003, after much thought and discussion with other Muslims, I invited several local Muslim leaders to meet at a mosque. We decided to start an organization, which we called the Muslim Coalition of Connecticut, which would address these concerns. I was elected as its first president.

There were four areas that we decided to deal with in a process of 'counter radicalization', if you will. This is not a term we thought of at that time but it is a term that I feel can counter the forces that divide us now.

One: the Muslim community, particularly our youth, needed to feel a sense of community in America and to this end we would celebrate our important holidays together. This would help us, especially our youth, develop a positive identity both as Americans and as Muslims.

Two: we wanted to change the perception of Muslims in America. We would do this through active engagement and outreach to other faith communities and having a speaker's bureau trained to speak on Islam and Muslims.

Three: we would live Islam through God-given guidance in the Qur'an; that is helping the poor and destitute through service and making this a priority of this organization.

Four: we would plan outreach events to let the public know who we are, and at those events we would answer any questions they had about Islam and Muslims as well.

We realized it would be too difficult to work through mosques alone for these goals. We needed an organization to bring together as much Muslim community involvement as was possible to proactively address these issues.

We addressed the first of our goals with the understanding that the Muslim community was negatively impacted by the events surrounding them. So we decided to have times when we could just have fun together. Muslims have two major celebrations called 'Eid' which means 'festival.' The first is after the month of fasting (known as 'Eid al Fitr') and the second is during the time of the pilgrimage, Hajj (known as 'Eid al Adha').

Ramadan, the month of fasting, is a rigorous time, in particular for the youth. The 'Eid' celebration, after the month of fasting, gives us an opportunity to enjoy a day in the comfort of our faith community. Fasting is not easy, but only those going through it can truly understand the spiritual impact that it has on the individual. We made arrangements to have our first celebration in a community park, and later, as our numbers increased, we moved to a theme park. The kids loved going to Lake Compounce or Six Flags, both of which were organized to have specially catered halal food for these celebrations. 'Halal' simply means 'permissible' and usually refers to meat and meat products. It is required that the animal be humanely treated and sacrificed with dignity for the consumption of its meat. We wanted American Muslims to feel that the U.S. was our home in every way and celebrating our festivals was one step in that direction. The Muslim Coalition of Connecticut has coordinated this 'Eid' celebration every year since our founding.

The festival of Hajj is a celebration of the performance of the pilgrimage, which really is associated with those who go on the pilgrimage to Makkah, in present day Saudi Arabia. In the Muslim Coalition of Connecticut we decided to celebrate this festival through outreach and education. So we had an event called the 'Footsteps of Abraham', where we shared food with guests from different towns. The 'Footsteps of Abraham' refers to the patriarch, Prophet Abraham's role as a unifying personality, as the father of monotheism, but also as the role model whose life we celebrate and whose sacrifices we contemplate during the Hajj pilgrimage.

Our second goal was to proactively define ourselves and to counter any negative portrayal of us. We felt that starting a speaker's bureau, with trained speakers on Islam and Muslims, would best achieve this. We wanted it to be as outreach-oriented as possible so that we use every opportunity to create an atmosphere of mutual understanding with people of other faiths. We spoke at churches and other places of worship, in hospitals and other institutions that wanted diversity training, including law enforcement agencies and the judiciary. We did not charge anything for these speaking engagements, although many organizations and faith communities paid small stipends to the speakers in gratitude.

Part of the outreach means getting involved in other organization's boards, so that we are active and contributing to society. Board members of the Muslim Coalition of Connecticut (MCCT) are encouraged to interact with other organizations. One such beautiful example of board members getting involved locally was in a school in downtown Hartford, Covenant Prep School, which was trying to help inner city kids who were good students and who had parental support. The school had a student-to-teacher ratio similar to a private school. Teachers were not paid but worked as a service to the community and funds were raised through local businesses to run the school. They invited me onto their board when I was the president of the Muslim Coalition of Connecticut and, as part of this, we started a program where a Muslim chaplain (Aida, my wife), a Christian pastor (Rev. Susan Izard) and a Jewish rabbi (Rabbi Debra Cantor) participated in making the curriculum so that children would learn about the major faith communities by a scholar from that faith. It was a wonderful success, as the students had an opportunity to really understand the three major monotheistic faiths represented. It is a beautiful model where sincere people were trying to make a difference.

I am not a fan of not teaching religion in schools because it has resulted in a generation of people who do not know anything about the major religions practiced all over the world. It has led to a vacuum of knowledge that needed to be filled, particularly after 9/11, and to fill this void about Islam we had to counter some awful characters with huge agendas who were speaking on our behalf.

The Connecticut Council for Inter religious Understanding (CCIU) is another organization that members of MCCT were a part of. CCIU includes leaders from nine faith communities who have united to show we can build bridges together. CCIU has also tried to alleviate the distrust that still exists among different faith communities. They organized the main post 9/11 cathedral service in Hartford, encouraging all the faith communities to stand united against the terror attacks on our nation. Since then, they have made public statements, organized movie screenings, and had dialogue groups inviting scholars of each faith community to address contemporary religion in America.

One particularly innovative idea was to invite the authors of "The Three Amigos: Getting to the Heart of Interfaith Dialogue" (Imam Jamal Rahman, Pastor Don Mackenzie, and Rabbi Ted Falcon) who spoke of building bridges of understanding together and writing about it.

We found that it was essential to be in dialogue and address issues of mutual concern. We have MCCT board members on town clergy organizations working on faith related issues that apply to all of us. As a result of this, during Thanksgiving services, Muslims were very much a part of the diversity of faith groups represented.

An organization that we are really proud to be a part of is Hartford Seminary. It is an institution that prides itself on preparing students to understand and live in today's multi-faith world. Soon after I was elected president of the Muslim Coalition of Connecticut, I got a call from the president of Hartford Seminary, inviting me to join the seminaries board of trustees. I was initially torn because at that time the Seminary had faculty who were not Muslim, teaching Islam, and I felt that such teachers would not be able to deliver the spirit of the message of Islam. I had obviously been affected by all the 'so called' scholars writing Op-Ed's on Islam with no knowledge of the religion, portraying Islam very negatively.

I weighed my concerns against the knowledge that Islam is being taught by non-Muslims in many university divinity schools in the United States of America, and that I could do more on the board, if I saw an obvious inaccuracy, than if I was not. Furthermore, there was an influx of Muslim students coming to Hartford Seminary at that time due to the need for more Muslim scholars, so there was an obvious need for some of us to be on the board, overseeing the direction of the institution as well as participating in the wellbeing of the institution.

There were now more jobs available for scholars of Islam in the prison system, hospitals, universities and the military. Muslim chaplains, in particular, were in high demand. I liked the concept of the chaplaincy program where Muslims, many of them born in this country, could represent their religion and be trained to be leaders of their communities. As I have illustrated before, I had some concerns about foreign Imams giving sermons in mosques in America, because there was a relevancy gap. There was also a dynamically changing and challenging environment that needed understanding and careful discernment.

It was not that the Imams coming from overseas were not well educated, in fact, many of them were very well educated, but if we had Imams trained in the United States they would understand the American environment much better. So, after weighing the pros and cons, I decided to accept the position on the board of trustees and have risen to the position of its first vice-chair.

The Seminary represents an oasis of hope for me. The interfaith dialogue is extremely respectful. It has a strong Muslim-Christian section, the 'Duncan Black McDonald Center for the Study of Islam and Christian Muslim Relations', and also a strong Jewish presence on the board, plus a recent increase in Jewish faculty, with a newly endowed chair in Abrahamic relations. In fact, the last chair of the board of trustees was Jewish and the present second vice-chair of the board is also Jewish. This shows a deep spiritual maturity in the Christian community at the Seminary in particular, and in Connecticut in general. It is very much in keeping with the understanding we have of Jesus, the wonderful human being, messenger of divine revelation, and the Messiah that the

Muslims accept him to be. His life reflects the loving acceptance of diversity and caring for the other that is enlightening.

Some board members of the Muslim Coalition of Connecticut were invited to be on the board of the American Civil Liberties Union, addressing our civil rights concerns and working to bridge the gap between our nation's civil rights organizations and the Muslim national civil rights organization, the Council on American Islamic Relations, CAIR. Many of our board members serve also as board members on mosque boards, and on the board of CAIR-Connecticut chapter. We needed to use as much of our resources within our local Islamic organizations while working outside of our community to have the maximum involvement in the process of outreach and dialogue.

Chapter 13

One Thousand Open Houses

Through the speakers bureau of the Muslim Coalition of Connecticut and individually, through our own alliances, we were getting lots of requests to come and speak. The settings of dialogue included religious and educational institutions, state agencies and private organizations that wanted to improve their diversity awareness. In particular, after 9/11 there was a thirst for knowledge about the true faith of Islam and it was important we provided that. The biggest challenge was countering the media bias.

Although we were always welcomed warmly, the attendees asked tough questions, including the concept of *Jihad*, women's role in Islam, Jesus in Islam, and the concept of *Shariah*. I explain all of this in the appendix section at the end of the book for the reader's perusal.

As we spoke more frequently, we incorporated these topics into our prepared remarks, prior to a question and answer session. We reserved the most time for the Q and A part. What is always inspiring to me are the comments after these open house events. Often, over a cup of tea or coffee, many people would say that they had learned in one evening what the media had confused them about over many years.

In other parts of the country we found 'love your neighbor' was not a part of their day-to-day lived experience. We got bigoted statements from people like Rev. Franklin Graham, the son of Rev. Billy Graham, who called Islam "wicked and evil". He attributed to Islam the evil of extremists, the worst of cultural (not Islamic) practices and also cherry picked and misquoted verses of the Qur'an, giving a false impression of the religion.

Similarly, Rev. Pat Robertson has also made very hurtful and disparaging statements about Islam based on the same factors as Graham. Robertson has gone one step further, saying that fighting Muslims is just like fighting Nazis. Opinions like this show a sense of insecurity in his religious conviction, and attacking Islam is the way he counters his fears and prejudices.

I believe Graham and Robertson, both Christians, go against the spirit of the beautiful message Jesus preached, and this is true of some clerics of all faiths here in the U.S., but also all over the world, including some Muslim clerics. Their attitudes are based on the belief that if you think you are right, you have the right to hurt and insult anyone who believes differently. It is certainly not the way of the messengers who brought divine revelation from God to us.

I believe that if God wanted only one faith to exist, there would be no other faiths here on earth. In His infinite wisdom, He chose instead to have this competition in good works between us of different faiths. So let us embrace that concept and compete in good works as, with respect and wisdom, we learn about each other.

The results of this dialogue, at least in Islam, are in God's hand and that divorces us from the immense responsibility of conversion, which some people fear is the only reason why Muslims come to conversation. It is God who does the 'converting'. The prophet was commanded by God to simply deliver the message, in numerous verses of the Qur'an, and not worry about the results. As Muslims, we have no greater a responsibility than the prophet had.

We found the Episcopal and Congregational churches to be the most open to dialogue, but there were notable others, including St. Patrick and St. Anthony Catholic Church in Hartford. They went out of their way to reach out to us and we were immensely grateful for that hospitality.

If you are not a Muslim, drop by a mosque or an Islamic center or ask a Muslim you know how you can be a part of the healing through your place of worship or organization or even individually. You will find our mosque administrations are open, to different degrees of outreach and dialogue, some certainly more than others. Below I have mentioned many different opportunities we took advantage of to get to know each other and, believe me, they spread more love and good will than we could have imagined.

These open houses were not only in churches, they were in synagogues and other places of worship, where we were invited to speak. We reciprocated by inviting their members to the mosque, where we now have regular open house events.

The Foundation for Ethnic Understanding together with the Islamic Society of North America and the World Jewish Congress organized a 'mosque-synagogue twinning program' in which, around the Thanksgiving weekend, we went to a local synagogue and they would reciprocate by visiting a mosque. We would have a dialogue between each other and end by having a meal together. The first event in Connecticut was held between the Islamic Association of Greater Hartford and Temple Beth David in Cheshire in 2008. It was held at the synagogue where I was invited to speak during the main Thanksgiving service on the scourge of Anti-Semitism and Islamophobia.

The discussion afterwards centered on our common values and it was very exciting to see just how much we had in common with Jews, even in theology. There is monotheism, prayer, fasting, giving in charity and a day of account (the latter at least with Orthodox Jews). Reform Jews do not believe in an afterlife when God will judge our deeds. We, Jews, Christians and Muslims also believe in angels, the Hebrew prophets, and divine revelation.

We realize that the politics around the State of Israel has caused a lot of friction, and that we all have to do more to work on maintaining our friendship and dialogue as a result. That conflict has left both communities bruised and this must be overcome through dialogue and a spirit of understanding, but that does not negate speaking about the injustices in the Holy Land, as standing against injustice and oppression is a universal value in all our faiths and a requirement at least in Islam.

The Israeli-Palestinian conflict is not the first topic I would choose to discuss when you first meet, but once a healthy relationship has been achieved, certain aspects can be addressed, with ground rules of engagement.

Another important thing we did was to involve our youth in this process of healing, through visits to churches and synagogues. Youth of the same age have a much easier time mixing, but we found that they avoid discussing religion. It was not 'cool' to discuss religion at that age. In addition, as it was obviously an area of misperceptions, it was too heavy for their agenda.

At these events, with the supervision and help of adults, they began to have discussions about each other's faith and came to understand each other better. Once again our impression, at the end, was how much we have in common with each other. Even our youth realized this.

We visited synagogues in Hamden, Cheshire and Newington. Sometimes these relationships went a step further than we originally planned, as in the case of the visit to the Hamden synagogue. The youth synagogue visit was followed by a visit to a museum about an Albanian village where Jews had been hidden and given protection from the Nazis by the local Muslim community. The Albanian people had a strong religious and cultural moral obligation to help the oppressed and that was why they did this. The Rabbi of the Hamden synagogue, Herbert Brockman, organized the museum tour. He saw this as an important step in breaking down the barriers between us.

The Newington synagogue experience happened because a congregant, Rita Miller, became friends with my wife. They decided to visit each other's place of worship and from there, a beautiful friendship between our two congregations blossomed. During such meetings we discussed theme topics from 'food and fasting' to 'marriage and divorce' to 'death and dying'. Each meeting reminds us that Jewish values through 'Halachic' law, and Islamic values through the guidance of Shariah, are extremely similar. We have deep common roots, of course, from common prophets to divine revelation in the form of books, including the Torah, which Muslims believe was originally revealed to Moses.

It was of paramount importance that our youth were learning about true religious cooperation and the benefits of it. They also learned the value of standing firm for justice and truth, for moral and ethical values as people of faith, and against genocide and evil at every level.

We were embraced by the other faith communities and invited frequently to address them. As people got to know who we are, they asked us to come back. It happened throughout the state and in the Greater Hartford area in particular.

The more we were known, the more the media now wanted us to comment on stories involving Islam. Many of my colleagues -

doctors, nurses, cleaning personnel, and security guards teased me about seeing my name or picture on the news or in the papers frequently. Many people have told me that knowing and hearing a Muslim has changed their impression of Muslims significantly. I would often be asked for my opinion on issues in the news by colleagues, friends and patients at work.

I heard "Really I am beginning to distrust the media more and more on how they depict Islam and Muslims" from many colleagues.

One Cardiac surgeon, Phil Almendinger joked, "Instead of cluttering our newspapers, why don't you just write a book?" He has since retired, but little did he know how seriously I took his challenge!

Islam challenged us to be the best we could be and to make society a better place and now that was happening, locally. Ultimately all these events and encounters humanized us, as Muslims. The best antidote to the kind of fear being spread about us is to be known.

There was more to come. Board members of MCCT got involved in hospital chaplaincy advisory boards, speaking in hospitals to staff about better understanding the Muslim patient and what it means to be a Muslim. We talked about Islamic medical ethics and issues pertaining to end of life and the concept of death in Islam.

We were blessed to have Muslim chaplains trained at Hartford Seminary as well as local Imams visit patients who were sick. Many helped pray at patient's bedsides, which gave them immense solace at this time of great need.

We spoke to social workers about Islam and the need to understand that we, in the Muslim Coalition of Connecticut, were here as a resource to help with these issues.

Each time we spoke, we were received with open arms as, in this case, health care professionals genuinely wanted to know our perspective concerning life and death so that healthcare workers could deliver better care. It made a huge difference to the Muslim patient to hear about end of life issues in Islam from a Muslim.

In 2015 we started an "honest conversations" project where the Muslim Coalition of Connecticut, together with the Connecticut Council for Inter-religious Understanding and Hartford Seminary had local churches and synagogues invite Muslim panels for an honest conversation to counter the huge amount of fear that is prevalent. Apart from brief introductory comments, the rest of the two hours is spent with the audience asking us any questions that they wanted to about Islam and Muslims. We have had about fifteen of these honest conversations, in various places of worship, and the attendance has been encouraging. People have fears and concerns, and how best to answer their concerns than an open discussion about our faith, with honesty? There are differences between what we believe in but that is no reason to fear each other or worse still vilify and hate each other. That type of thinking comes from an extremely immature and insecure person, whatever faith they belong to.

As a result of all this involvement, MCCT became a vibrant organization, dynamic in its outlook. What is more, we have near equal representation of both genders and an active youth presence on our board, which keeps us vital.

Our goal is to be able to keep our religious values and individuality while fully participating in society. We are proud of our Islamic heritage and values while, at the same time, we are proud of this nation that stands for many of the values Muslims hold dear, including the values of freedom, liberty and the individual rights that are enshrined in our nation's laws. This is in truth the very reason many of us came to America, and before us, many of your ancestors did too. We are certainly extremely grateful for that opportunity.

Chapter 14

Doors Keep Opening

Public libraries responded to the open houses by holding discussions on Islam and Muslims. The Hartford Public Library was the most proactive. It held civil rights and immigration forums and invited someone from the Muslim community, usually the Muslim Coalition of Connecticut (MCCT), to the discussion.

In one forum, they hosted a civil rights expert, an immigration lawyer, a member of the Department of Homeland Security, and me. The subject was 'The American Muslim Experience'. It was well attended and the audience came out of it understanding that Muslims were struggling to make it in the United States, just as previous immigrant communities had done, but that we had the added burden of scrutiny by national security and having to contend with hateful rhetoric as well. That forum humanized our struggles with immigration issues on top of national security issues and made others aware that coming here was a rocky landing for Muslims who simply wanted to attempt to achieve the American Dream.

The public libraries received a grant in 2012 to study Islamic diversity by reviewing books and documentary type movies about Islam and Muslim cultures throughout the world. It is called the 'Bridging Cultures Bookshelf' and involves over 800 libraries throughout the nation.

The Connecticut libraries invited speakers from MCCT to head the discussion groups. Aida became heavily involved, as she is a community Muslim chaplain, and was very well trained in doing exactly that. She has often told me about the wonderful people who organize and attend these events. Books were chosen on understanding the faith of Islam, on different Muslim cultures and practices, and on the challenges we face as Muslims. Often they would discuss the challenges of women, for example in Afghanistan, and contrast their struggles due to what the pervasive culture dictates compared to what Islam allows. For example, education of women and men is compulsory in Islam but this clashed culturally with what was 'allowed' and sometimes it was thought to be Islam that put these restrictions on them.

The library grant that made these exchanges possible came from the Carnegie Corporation of New York, the Doris Duke Foundation for Islamic Art, and the National Endowment for the Humanities. These were very well recognized charitable institutions and therefore opposition to this initiative, although present, was relatively muted.

The Avon Public School District has an annual interfaith discussion, and in 2011, it was on 'Genocide and Forgiveness'.

Where they had in the past only invited Christians of different denominations and Jews, in 2011 they invited me as well. They had heard from other teachers about MCCT and what we do and wanted our perspective on this important topic.

When it was my turn to speak, I reminded them that throughout history, all of our faith communities have had some renegades who have done horrendous evil, and we have all also been the victims of horrendous evil.

It was therefore in the best interest of all of us to educate one another on what leads to genocide. I explained that it does not start suddenly or in a vacuum. It starts with a few people who falsely attribute evil stereotypes to people of other races or religions and once dehumanized, it is easier to scapegoat them and act violently towards them, the ultimate outcome being genocide. Unless the silent majority acts to prevent the steps that lead to genocide, it is very difficult to halt the hatred, once it has a momentum of its own.

We must therefore be vigilant about the steps that lead to stereotyping, including students who are name-called and the subject of bullying. It is vital that bullying be stopped and the perpetrators be shown that there is something very wrong indeed in their thinking. We must also watch for and stop adults from irrational hate of minority groups and acts of aggression based on racism and bigotry, because this is very much akin to bullying.

My message was appreciated by the young students who asked me many questions. I hope they will become the future warriors for peace and coexistence. Older teens want to know how to be involved in solving the problems we face and we should encourage them to take on the mantle of healing and peacemaking. I have a lot of confidence in their abilities to make this a more vibrant and inclusive world.

On the issue of forgiveness, I explained that Muslims start everything we do with the name of the One God, the Most Forgiving and Compassionate, the Most Merciful. Therefore, we are constantly reminded of God's abundant mercy and forgiveness, as these are the most important attributes of God. We speak those words before eating, leaving our homes, or initiating any new venture; in fact we say it before anything we do.

I explained that the Islamic version of the story of the creation and eviction from heaven of Adam and Eve, is associated with God forgiving them and therefore, in Islam, we are all born free of sin. We must look to the awesome examples of Jesus who said, 'turn the other cheek,' thus showing his followers that forgiveness means not retaliating, and to Muhammad who forgave all his enemies during the conquest of Makkah, the city he was forced to leave due to the constant attacks, showing us, his followers, exactly the same thing.

Prophet Muhammad told his companions, and through them all of us. "Be Merciful to those on earth so that the Most Merciful One in heaven may be merciful to you?" His advice on another occasion was, "Do not be people without minds of your own, saying that if others treat you well, you will treat them well and that if they wrong you, you will wrong them. But (instead) accustom yourselves to doing good if people do good to you or not."

The challenge now is for the Muslim communities across the country to organize events where they get to meet people of other faiths, especially the youth, and to convey these teachings.

We must not forget the Qur'an says, "God does not change the condition of a people until they change themselves". There has to be a change of mindset within ourselves for God to help us and we have to be proactive in changing the narrative. We have to make a positive contribution to get a positive response from God – that is the Islamic understanding.

We are blessed in Connecticut with faith leadership that wants to reach out and work to have better relations.

As the founding president of MCCT, I have been interviewed many times on radio and TV stations. The interviews that really made a difference were the ones on National Public Radio, NPR, as they gave me enough time to explain concepts. John Dankosky has interviewed me several times, as has Collin McEnroe; both are phenomenal interviewers. They do their homework and are knowledgeable about the topics they discuss, thus imparting a great deal of education to the public.

Television interviews on the other hand are rarely more than sound bites. On NPR, I could go into more depth. For example I explained the Muslim position regarding the Park51 issue (explained later), and whenever friends and acquaintances met me after that, they would make it a point to tell me that what I had said had made a significant difference in their understanding of the Muslim perspective.

It hasn't always been easy. I was once called up by the producer of the *Chaz and AJ Show* and was told that my moderate voice, as a Muslim, was what needed to be heard and would I come on their show at 7am one day. Trusting the producer's explanation regarding the need for a moderate voice, I did not even research them and agreed to go on their show. I realized very quickly, during the interview, that I was there so they could insult and make fun of Muslims to improve their ratings. They compared what I had for breakfast with what the Time Square bomber had eaten, for example. Finally they asked me what I did for a living and as soon as I said I was a cardiologist, their tone changed completely. I had broken their stereotype. They became very respectful and ended the interview quickly.

It really is quite amazing how the extremist worldview is based on stereotypes and that they don't give you a chance unless they feel you are a 'somebody'. Every human being should be given the benefit of respect unless he loses it by his or her words or actions.

Chapter 15

Living Islam - Serving Humanity

Our third reason for establishing the Muslim Coalition of Connecticut (MCCT) was to live by doing what Islam asked of its adherents with a deep focus on social equity and justice. We are strongly encouraged:

a.   to give to the poor, the orphan and wayfarer,
b.   to help the traveler and the homeless,
c.   to right the social diseases that prevent all of us from being productive citizens.

To accomplish this, we participate in serving in soup kitchens and shelters monthly, building habitat houses regularly, and joined the walk against hunger sponsored by 'Foodshare' annually, all done under the aegis of the Muslim Coalition of Connecticut.

We include our youth in each of these efforts, which helps them to understand our shared values as Americans and Muslims. We make it a priority to take them with us on projects which demonstrate that we must look after those less fortunate than ourselves.

Cooking and serving in soup kitchens is, from an Islamic perspective, a very meritorious deed, and there was never a shortage of people willing to cook and serve. In fact, it was not uncommon for us to have too many people helping out. People in the shelters loved the Middle Eastern and Asian food we made because it was different and very flavorful and they enthusiastically told us so.

As a community, we felt a debt of gratitude to the United States for all that we have been able to achieve here. Serving the poor feels like we have a means to give back, it made us feel good. We try to provide a hearty and healthy meal for every person who comes to the shelter in the inner city of Hartford and we want to expand our involvement to feed people in cities throughout Connecticut.

We invited other faith communities to join us in serving and building (Habitat for Humanity houses), building bridges of friendship while serving the needy. We took interfaith dialogue to the next level – service to humanity as people of faith. It was not just words, but action and social justice oriented work, through the calling of all our faiths.

Rebecca Minor and Aida, both board members of MCCT, coordinate the social service work we do. They have invited church groups to join us and among those who have joined are St. Patrick and St. Anthony Church in Hartford, the Connecticut Council for Inter-religious Understanding and many other places of worship. All of this has made a huge difference in how we are viewed locally. It is this 'open house' grassroots action that was needed to dispel the ugly myths about us.

As helping the poor is a requirement in all our traditions, we supported and worked on a novel 'open house' model. Habitat for Humanity in Connecticut started having builds with innovative themes. One such build involved the three Abrahamic faiths (the monotheistic faiths that have Abraham as their spiritual father). The 'House of Abraham', project had Jews, Christians and Muslims working together and all contributed financially towards a house being built in the inner city of Hartford. We, in MCCT, were eager to participate fully in the build, because it was in keeping with our Islamic tradition of helping the poor and dispossessed. We also knew our young population would be interested in doing something positive for the poor.

We contributed $10,000 towards the first house, as we realized the importance of this endeavor, and had large numbers of young adults participate in the build. As part of this project, Habitat wanted us to coordinate speaker events in each other's places of worship, to get to know one another. With each house that was built we, therefore, had an outreach event in a Jewish, Christian and Muslim place of worship. During these events we spoke from each faith perspective about what our religions taught us regarding helping the poor. We built houses while building closer bonds of friendship and bridges of understanding getting to know each other better in particular our huge commonalities and small differences. Our three religions have much more in common than divide us, if we only took the courage to get to know each other.

Although we have disagreements in some aspects, theologically, we are respectful of the differences, as we understand that God has created diversity in religion for a purpose. We also acknowledged that historically, at times, we have vilified each other. All of our religions are guilty of this. Accepting this helped those who attended recommit, understanding that we have no recourse but to work with each other to make our nation a better place. We have to address the important issues of homelessness, poverty and the other social ills our nation faces. The sooner we trust each other and work together the better off we will all be, not only as a community in Hartford, but also as a nation. We must first come to the conclusion that we are in this together.

We ended each program with a sumptuous meal organized by the host faith community. We thus got to know our neighbors and got to humanize each other. The bridges that have been built are meant to withstand the stereotyping of each other no matter how much media induced confusion there is, and it has served that purpose.

MCCT members also coordinated the *'Foodshare'*, 'Walk Against Hunger' Muslim team, called 'Muslims Against Hunger'. We made it fun for the youth giving out free T-shirts and got together the largest faith community team that walked in Hartford – raising a large amount of money for *Foodshare*.

One of the full time Islamic schools in Connecticut, Madina Academy, encouraged us by sending large teams of students to walk with us. All of this debunked the stereotype that Muslims are aloof and isolated from the rest of America. We fought all stereotypes by encouraging our community to get involved actively and not just through words.

Another novel way we worked together was for environmental awareness, after an MCCT annual banquet on the theme 'Islam and our Environmental Responsibility'. We joined with the Inter-religious Eco-Justice Network, IREJN, who had been one of the awardees at our leadership banquet and participated, not only in highlighting the importance of environmental responsibility together, but also in building bridges of friendship while doing that. We went on hikes with them appreciating in nature God's beauty and reflected on what humanity is doing to destroy our habitats. Terri Eikel, the executive director of IREJN, educated the Muslim community on issues, such as the importance of solar power as a source of energy, to protect the environment. MCCT actively participated, even having a member of MCCT on the IREJN board and in organizing many of their outreach efforts to the community.

Chapter 16

September 2010 and Park 51

2010, after the initial challenges in the immediate aftermath of 9/11, was our most difficult year. The atmosphere around September 11th 2010, the ninth anniversary of the attacks, was very disheartening. As Muslims, we felt we had been making progress in defining ourselves and other Americans seemed to be getting to know us better, at least that was true in Connecticut. But then the controversy around the Park51 Cultural Center erupted and it coincided with the mid-term elections. Whenever there is an election, opportunistic politicians say some pretty awful things, stereotyping and scapegoating 'the other', as they try to play on people's fears (based on polls), while making themselves look strong. These are the most dangerous politicians and we must beware of their successes, because it is a harbinger of problems for our future.

The Park 51 Cultural Center was the idea of a Muslim developer named Sharif Al Gamal and was to include a prayer space for Muslims. The place he chose had been initially named Cordoba House and the site was chosen because a large Arab American population, many of them Muslim, live there. It was several blocks away from where the 9/11 attacks took place; the attack site now known as 'ground zero'.

Pamela Geller, the co-founder of 'Stop Islamization of America', and a well recognized and credentialed Islamophobe, took this opportunity to begin a whole new controversy, and dragged Islam and Muslims through the mud with it. She called the building "The Ground Zero Mega Mosque" which naturally conjured up fear and linked that to the memory of those who died on 9/11, suggesting that those who had died on that tragic day were being dishonored through this project.

To explain the issues surrounding the downtown Park51 Cultural Center better, here are a few not very well known facts. Downtown Manhattan, around this area, was known as "Little Syria" due to the number of Arab immigrants that had come there in the early 20th century. Rather than having to walk blocks away, to an area where they did not live in, they wanted to build a place of worship where their congregation lived.

The decision had nothing to do with 'triumphalism' as claimed by Pamela Geller, but simply to do with building a place of worship close to where many adherents of that faith lived.

To say that a mosque desecrates the sanctity of Ground Zero, even though the building was not at 'Ground Zero', was an obvious insult, meant to hurt us. It also negated the lives of the many Muslims who died during that awful day, including among them many Muslim 'first responders'.

As Geller spread her hate, bringing out the worst in humanity, we experienced a new surge of discrimination, violence and hate crimes. She did this while standing with an American flag, portraying herself as this patriotic freedom fighter for America while trying to destroy the delicate fabric of tolerance this nation is known for. This was the same abuse of patriotism that religious extremists use when they quote Holy Scripture to justify wars and killings. Patriotism is a powerful tool which can be used with devastating effect, as is religion, when abused by haters.

In many ways what was happening was reminiscent of the intolerance of a few arch hate-mongers before the civil war in Sri Lanka. Before civil wars there are extremists who go around fanning the flames of hatred. They are masters at what they do and seem to have studied their effects well. They are very insecure people with paranoid fears that need addressing.

The negative publicity around the protests against the Park51 Cultural Center were reported abroad and then backfired. It created anger against the United States in Muslim countries in the Arab world and beyond. This kind of action of hatred is how hate gets spread and then we wonder why do *they* hate us? Once the substrate of hatred is created, you only need a little incident to ignite the violence that then engulfs the region, whether that is Libya or elsewhere.

At home a different problem evolved. The grotesque protests against Park 51 she ignited spread to other parts of the country. It resulted in prejudice against mosques being built from Tennessee to

California. As the protesters could not just protest having mosques at these sites, due to the First Amendment, they used parking and traffic concerns as the issue to oppose the mosque projects with.

The Catch-22 is that those who oppose the construction of mosques complain that we overcrowd and over-park in the mosques that exist. It is obvious that that is the reason we need more places of worship, not less. But that is the exact reason they give as the reason we should not be given permission to build more places of worship. It makes no sense but it has worked in some places.

National Public Radio interviewed me in August 2010 to explain the Muslim position regarding Park 51[21]. I explained to them what I have illustrated above, reiterating the need for more understanding and tolerance of one another. I also explained the need for all of us to stop listening to the voices that aim to divide us and propagate hate, which is not an American value; it is instead what we all came to America to get away from.

Many who heard this program called me after it to tell me that I had made a big difference in their understanding of the issues involved. They said I had explained the issues objectively and without the emotions and anger that they had heard from some others in other interviews.

But the rhetoric against Islam and Muslims was having an effect this year, and once again our youth were struggling with verbal abuse and bullying in schools. In Bridgeport, Connecticut, a Christian church group visited from Texas and according to

[21] http://www.yourpublicmedia.org/content/wnpr/where-we-live-mosques-and-islam-america

witnesses they called out "Murderers!" at the children going to pray at a local mosque, in an obvious reference to 9/11. Do they believe Jesus would have approved of that? Would he have gone out on missions like this, against innocent children?

For Muslims, the Qur'an speaks extremely reverentially about this great messenger of the Gospel that we know he would never partake in hate. We know that Jesus would never have supported the burning of books of guidance or hurting anyone, especially children.

The Qur'an burning incident by Rev. Terry Jones of Florida was further proof that those who wanted to use religion to spread hate and not love, were thriving in this environment. Once again, far from the teachings of Jesus, the Messiah and messenger Muslims know him and love him for.

Around September 11th 2010, the Hartford City Council invited a local Imam from Hartford to give the opening prayer prior to the city council meeting. Imam Kashif is a descendent of slaves, who converted to Islam after hearing the message of universal brotherhood, which left no room for racism.

A local radio talk show host decided to make this invitation an issue and started telling people to call the City Council and demand a retraction of this invitation. The leader of the City Council caved in, due to the pressure on her, and retracted the invitation. This was a direct insult to Muslims, as it associating the terror attacks of 9/11 to the religion of Islam and all Muslims. Unfortunately, it was an insult that was becoming more common.

A few of us gathered outside City Hall in Hartford on the day Imam Kashif was supposed to give the opening prayer and we were joined by some legislators and the Imam delivered a somber prayer outside. We left saddened that the message of hate seemed to be winning out everywhere that year.

These four incidents, all around September 11th 2010, the ninth anniversary of the terrorist attacks, made us insecure. We had to think fast. The Muslim Coalition of Connecticut leadership in coordination with the leadership of the Muslim community decided to invite other faith community leaders to a press conference on the steps of the state capitol to speak about this matter. It was heartening to see clergy and lay leaders come from all over the state to support us.

Rabbi Eric Silver from Cheshire, CT spoke about the creeping stereotyping of Islam and Muslims in public discourse and said that it sounded very similar to Nazi Germany's treatment of the Jews. He compared the Qur'an burning and animosity to what happened in Germany prior to the concentration camps.

He said, "The burning of books, the burning of Jewish owned stores and the media's decision not to point out what was wrong directly resulted in the Holocaust".

Coming from a Rabbi, these were powerful words.

The inter-religious partnerships with other faith leaders that allowed for such a press conference had been built over many years. I had spoken about the similarities between Islamophobia and anti-Semitism at his synagogue a couple of years prior, in a synagogue-mosque 'twinning' event and that friendship allowed him to speak to us freely and supportively.

Through all the turmoil, the Muslim community was growing up fast. We had to rise to the challenge and offer hope where there was anger. A challenge we did not take lightly.

Chapter 17

Taking a Stand in Hartford

After a successful press conference with the clergy, we decided to invite politicians to a press conference at Hartford Seminary on 'Religious Intolerance and Islamophobia'. I chose Hartford Seminary as it has been an island of tolerance, teaching mutual respect and shared values through all of our faith traditions.

I called the president of the seminary, Dr. Heidi Hadsell, and asked her for permission to hold the event at the Seminary. She welcomed us to go ahead and make arrangements to have the press conference there, as she felt that it was in keeping with the mission of the seminary.

We called, e-mailed and faxed the candidates running for governor and the senate in 2010 and they all gave excuses as to why they could not be there or more often simply ignored our request. Only one candidate, an independent for the senate could make it! We were stunned at this response as we thought attending a rally against religious intolerance should have been a no-brainer.

We had to ask ourselves, if this was a press conference on anti-Semitism and religious intolerance organized by the Jewish or Christian community, would they have gotten the same response?

Rabbi Herbert Brockman from Hamden and Reverend David Good from Old Lyme delivered the Jewish and Christian response. They were good friends of mine and gladly accepted the invitation to speak.

I first met Rabbi Brockman when we were on a panel against the death penalty in the United States and have been working together since then on many important issues. The Islamic view on the death penalty is that it is permissible only under very strict guidelines and the most stringent of conditions.

My take on the death penalty is that the system in the United States is too ridden with faults for it to be a fair system. You may be surprised at that, but when the African American community is disproportionately affected, where a majority of death row inmates are from that community, and when there are a disproportionate number of death penalty convictions in the Southern states as opposed to the Northeast, it is a system that cannot be fair or just.

A proper penal code should be temporally and geographically identical, as the standard for taking a person's life for a crime must be absolutely foolproof. If we have the death penalty, then it should be completely just and until then it must be suspended. We cannot play around with people's lives.

Many Muslims came to me, after I stood at the Legislative Building of the State Capital and spoke against the death penalty, and asked me how I could stand up as a Muslim, representing Islam, and say I was opposed to the death penalty when Islam allows it for certain crimes.

I was clear in my reply; there are examples of the first caliphs, or successors of the prophet, abandoning the penal code in situations where there was a good reason to do so, including famine. As long as there is a degree of uncertainty either in the implementation of justice or in the certainty of the crime, Islam does not allow it. I feel the death penalty in the United States does not fit those stringent criteria. I understood full well that many Muslim countries do not follow Islam's stringent guidelines for the taking of life, but what is practiced in some parts of the Muslim world does not make it acceptable in Islam.

The injustice of slavery is the main reason for African Americans to be in the situation they are in. A third of all African American men have been incarcerated at some point in their lives. For a nation so advanced, it seems a tragedy that as a community we have not paid more attention to this injustice. I am also surprised that politicians have not taken this issue more seriously, as incarceration rates among African Americans suggests that they are being victimized again. This is a gross violation of justice as they were a people uprooted from West Africa and brought here as slaves against their will. We have taken away their past, and that surely has a huge impact on their upbringing and life, and it must be taken into account and addressed, without just throwing them in jail and taking away their future as well. It remains, by far, the darkest blemish in the history of humanity that we enslaved our own kind and often treated them as sub-human!

Reverend David Good, the Christian speaker at the press conference was a very humble and just leader. He was the senior minister of Old Lyme Congregational Church and a person who, in the footsteps of Jesus, wanted to be a witness against injustice. He had been to the Holy Land, several times, and felt that keeping quiet about the occupation and brutal treatment of the Palestinians in the occupied territories was unconscionable and, therefore, every year he organizes a "Tree of Life" Conference and invites Jews, Christians, and Muslims to speak as witnesses to the injustice of the occupation in the Holy Land.

I had asked him to be the Christian speaker, as he had written an Op-Ed on Islamophobia, illustrating the solution to this 'disease'[22]. His prescription was for people to get to know a Muslim. He went on to humanize Muslims, by describing several of his Muslim friends in this Op-Ed. I was honored to have been mentioned as one of his friends and consider him a dear friend of mine. This human interaction and humanization of the other is the solution to the problem of Islamophobia, he wrote. I completely agree with his analysis.

Both Rabbi Brockman and Rev. Good spoke very powerfully and there were others, particularly Carole Fay from St. Patrick and St. Anthony Church in Hartford, who gave stirring accounts of their enlightening experiences working with the Muslim community. A

---

[22] http://www.sailanmuslim.com/news/solution-to-islamophobia-by-david-w-good/

few Hartford City Council representatives showed up, perhaps out of a feeling of guilt, for what had happened to the Imam, and to listen to the Imam, who gave the opening prayer here as well.

We realized that we had not built bridges with politicians, and realized that for politicians we had become a liability to support, and they were better off not associating with us. We realized also that the following year, the tenth anniversary after the terror attacks, could be a year when we could face an explosion of hate towards us.

The Muslim Coalition of Connecticut leadership decided that we would proactively start working to make arrangements to show that we, as a community, realize the pain of our country men and women. In showing our humanity we would be the ones who took a step in the direction of healing. We would start work immediately on coordinating the September 11th 2011 tenth anniversary memorial interfaith service.

Chapter 18

The Tenth Anniversary of 9/11

In March 2011, the Muslim Coalition of Connecticut, under its new leader Rabia Chaudry, a lawyer and mother of two beautiful girls, asked me to coordinate the memorial service to express our hope, and sincere need for healing, on this tenth anniversary of the terrorist attacks on our nation.

I invited many faith community leaders including:

-Catholic Bishop Peter Rosazza,

-Episcopal Bishop Ian Douglas,

-United Church of Christ interim minister Rev. Charles Wildman,

-Several congregational priests,

-Several Rabbis,

-The leadership of the Connecticut Council for Inter-religious Understanding, which was an organization that had representation from nine faith groups. In addition to Judaism, Christianity and Islam, they including:

-Hindus,
-Sikhs,
-Jains,
-Buddhists,

-Baha'is,
-Unitarian Universalists.

Representatives of other denominations and organizations who wanted to be part of the healing process in a memorial service, including the AFLCIO, the voluntary federation of 57 national and international labor unions, joined our efforts.

We invited them to meet with the Muslim leadership at the Islamic Association of Greater Hartford in Berlin, Connecticut. There was an open discussion on how we could bring healing to our communities now, a full decade after 9-11-01.

It was an extremely productive meeting. After introductions, I explained the need the Muslim community felt in coordinating this memorial service. Everyone knew the Muslim leadership was very serious about this, and nobody at the table voiced any objection to us organizing and coordinating such a service. This was the degree of maturity of the interfaith groups involved. They realized the need to play a supportive role in this process of healing for our state.

The Episcopal Bishop Ian Douglas went right to the point when he said: "Reza, we have so much work to alleviate fears from our community, with the economic collapse, to their houses not being worth anything, to the end of the world coming this year (which was a prediction, around March 2011), that anything we can do to alleviate fear is worth it. To have the Muslims coordinating this would reassure the community at large immensely and show that the Muslims seriously want healing and that what they hear of the Muslims from media sound bites was completely untrue. I vote 'yes'!"

His statement started a chorus of yea's and so began an amazing coalition of faith and other groups that wanted to be a part of the healing. Despite not being a faith based organization, the AFLCIO got on board, as did the Connecticut Center for a New Economy. We agreed, understanding full well that the more diverse our support was the better.

We now had a huge coalition of groups all putting their weight behind this event. It was decided at that meeting that the memorial interfaith service should have the flavor of all our faith communities while being reverential.

The Muslim community also decided that, in addition to the interfaith service on Sunday September 11th 2011, on the 10th of September, we would have open houses in as many mosques and Islamic Centers in the state of Connecticut as possible. Fourteen Islamic Centers in Connecticut participated. That was an impressive number as each center would be inviting their neighbors, politicians and neighboring faith communities to visit their center, organize something to eat for them, and prepare a program to let their neighbors know them better.

On September 10th 2011 I was at the Islamic Association of Greater Hartford where about 200 people, including my good friend Christopher Donovan, the Speaker of the House, attended the two hour meet-and-greet. I have great respect for Speaker Donovan, not only because he was a politician who stood up for important values that we both believed in, but he was not afraid to publicly stand with the Muslims who he believed in, despite the fact that this was unpopular. He supported universal health care for the millions of Americans that did not have it, he encouraged our role in standing as stewards for environmental responsibility and even had a task force to address domestic violence awareness; important priorities for both of us. I admired him for his strong stand on these issues. The Muslim Coalition of Connecticut, in trying to highlight all three of these issues through its banquets, found him to be a strong advocate.

While there are those who cynically say that politicians will join anybody just to get votes, in this case, joining with Muslims was generally considered toxic to getting votes. Getting politicians to stand with us was very difficult as we had learned the previous year when we invited many of them to rallies on religious tolerance.

From March 2011 we began a very sincere effort to try to involve as many faith communities to join us, with mainly positive results. The amazing thing about this effort was the unexpected consequences.

On one occasion to try to publicize our plans and hope to get the local newspaper to agree to write an editorial on our efforts, we met with the Editorial Board of the *Hartford Courant*. The conversation began with one of the Editorial Board members saying, "I really think this Islamophobia stuff is exaggerated. I don't see it!"

Her remark was directed at me, but Bishop James Curry, the Episcopal Suffragan Bishop, felt embarrassed for me at having to address this comment and therefore spoke up himself. He spoke very forcefully, illustrating all the different events that showed the degree of Islamophobia out there. He referenced the Qur'an burning incident, the vitriolic rhetoric around Park 51 - the Cultural Center near Ground Zero, the incident in Bridgeport where children were called murderers near a mosque, and the retracted prayer of the Imam at the Hartford City Council meeting, all around September 2010. I could not have said it more eloquently and they were sold on the idea and promised to write the editorial.

It was great working together. I wished more people in America could see religion in action in a positive way, instead of blaming it for all the problems and negativism in the world. When genuinely good-hearted people realize they are watching injustice, there is a strong urge to get off the sidelines and be heard and work to change that narrative. When that is done, there will be positive change. When it is religious people doing it, who are driven their whole lives with these positive values, it is all the more evident. We were witnessing this happen.

We decided that the memorial service would be held at the huge St. Joseph's Catholic Cathedral, in Hartford, as it could accommodate about 2,500 people on its main floor. It was also the location of the interfaith service that was held soon after the 9/11 terrorist attacks, in memory of the victims and their families. The Archbishop, Reverend Henry Mansell, opened the cathedral to us saying, "As long as it is not at a time of our service we will make every effort to assist and open our doors to you".

Father Michael Dolan was our point person from the Catholic Diocese, and was as sincere a friend as we could have. He made all the arrangements and even managed to get Edward Cummings, the retired maestro of the Hartford Symphony Orchestra, to coordinate some solemn as well as some uplifting music during intermissions between speakers.

The theme of the event was "United in Peace, Healing with Hope"[23]. The main coordinators of the actual service were the Episcopal Suffragan Bishop, Rev. James Curry, the United Church of Christ Interim Minister, Rev. Charles Wildman, and me.

The program began with the processional, accompanied by music from the Hartford Symphony Orchestra. It was very solemn and dignified. The processional was followed by a candle lighting event by the sister of one of the victims of the 9/11 terror attacks on the Twin Towers in New York.

The welcome and introduction was by Rebecca Minor, the secretary of MCCT, an articulate speaker and teacher in the Farmington school system. She is a direct descendent of one of the original Mayflower pilgrims and had accepted Islam as her religion and way of life when she was in College, at the University of Connecticut. As she was a woman, a convert to Islam, and a Caucasian, it broke the stereotype of Muslims being Arab men with accents, as usually portrayed in the movies.

Rebecca's introduction was followed by a welcome by the Archbishop who then introduced the other speakers, and became

---

[23] http://www.ccfiu.org/PDF/UnitedPeaceHealingHope-Sept11th.pdf

the master of ceremonies for the event. Each speaker and message had been deliberated over and planned meticulously.

There were prayers, chants, songs and speeches from native Indians, Sikhs, Hindus, Buddhists, Baha'is and of course the three Abrahamic faith community leaders. The theme was the need to unite in peace and heal and it was beautifully illustrated that evening.

Rabia Chaudry, the president of the Muslim Coalition of Connecticut for the year 2011 gave the speech on behalf of the Muslims. "As a faith community", she began, "we need to lead the way in healing and moving forward as a nation. For Muslims, our religion and prophet are our inspiration for this. We are looking forward to being an example of a community taking its responsibility seriously". Her message was much longer than that and was very well received, as were all the efforts the Muslim community made in helping organize the event and ensuring its success.

The conclusion of the event was powerful and memorable. The original candle was used by ushers to light candles given to every attendee. They lit their candle and so symbolically took the light of this message of healing to their communities far and wide. The symbolism was felt deeply by everyone who was there.

The Governor could not make it as he had many appointments that day. The Lieutenant Governor, Nancy Wyman, therefore attended in his place. As she entered I was introduced to her as the coordinator of the event. She exclaimed, "This is very interesting, a

Jewish Lieutenant Governor, attending a service in a Catholic cathedral, organized by a Muslim!"

Only in America, it seemed, was this degree of cooperation possible through a genuine and heartfelt need to be the solution to a problem created by extremists from outside of our nation. This is the beauty of what interfaith relations should be, and I sincerely believe this is the best in tolerance and understanding of one another. Understanding the pain and expressing our sincere concern is the key here. The Muslim community needed to be able to do this with foresight, wisdom and sincerity. We succeeded in doing that and what an awesome evening it was.

Other dignitaries in attendance included Pedro Segarra, the mayor of Hartford, John Larson, the U.S. Congressman for the 1st district, where this was held, and United States Senator, Richard Blumenthal. The cathedral was packed with members of the public who just wanted to be a witness, pay their respects and remember the victims.

This event changed many things locally. Everyone who participated felt a sense of great camaraderie. The Muslims locally were seen as healers and peacemakers reminding us of the prophet's words when he entered Medina, after being expelled from Makkah: "Be a people that are known for spreading peace and feeding people...". His advice was to become known as the peacemakers of the lands you move to. We were attempting to do that.

The environment that had been created was so positive that the local chapter of the AFLCIO even went as far as to invite the Muslim community to the next AFLCIO Annual Convention. On September 14th 2011 they passed Resolution 7 "Condemning anti-Muslim bigotry and discrimination". It was approved *unanimously.*

It read as follows:

"Whereas, ten years ago, on September 11th, Muslims were not only among those killed, they were among the first responders who died trying to save others, and; whereas, there is a growing and dangerous trend of anti-Muslim sentiment and bigotry that has developed and intensified since 9/11 and; whereas such discrimination creates barriers to full participation by Muslims in public life and in the workplace; whereas Muslims are everyday Americans and workers and among our union brothers and sisters and; whereas Muslims have been part of the diverse fabric of this nation since its founding and; whereas Muslim institutions and organizations are on record saying that they condemn terrorism and defend this country with many serving in the armed services and; whereas, religion can be used as a political wedge to divide workers who otherwise would be united and; whereas this country was founded on the principles of religious freedom and tolerance and these principles are embraced by the labor movement and; whereas silence about intolerance and discrimination diminishes the voices that will speak up for the labor movement that is under attack and; therefore be it resolved that the Connecticut AFL-CIO honor the memory of our citizens who died on 9/11 by condemning discrimination and bigotry that runs contrary to our founding principles; therefore be it further resolved that the Connecticut AFL-CIO be a leader in educating and participating in activities that build bridges among diverse groups of Americans and that break down discrimination and intolerance towards Muslims; therefore be it further resolved that the Connecticut AFL-CIO support the week of peace and reconciliation that is sponsored by a broad coalition of religious community organizations and be it finally resolved that the Connecticut AFL-CIO urge the national AFL-CIO to support national legislation and activities that protect our Muslim union brothers and sisters from discrimination and bigotry."

A small act of healing had started creating unintended ripples of a very positive nature, and we were making so many friends along the way.

I realized this would not have come about had we not brought the AFL-CIO on board by meeting with them beforehand and explaining the benefits of the healing event that we had planned.

I had met with its president, John Olsen, in February of 2011 and explained to him what the Muslim community had in mind for the September 11th 2011 memorial service. I explained that we wanted the service to be as ecumenical as possible and asked him if he would be able to bring the first responder community to the service. The police, for example, were part of that union. I also asked if the AFLCIO would co-sponsor this event and explained that it would not require any financial burden but would require participation in the service.

He had me make a presentation to his board. They unanimously agreed to participate and co-sponsor the event. John Olsen, as president, then attended most of the organizational meetings and contributed fully to the success of the event, realizing the genuineness of our endeavor and our sincerity in bringing about reconciliation. He was, in the true American spirit of outreach, truly patriotic by inclusion and adhering to our national principles of tolerance.

This I believe is the best of America. I sincerely believe that most Americans, when explained the truth of who we are and what we are about, will want to work with us in furthering the goals of understanding one another. Then they will not allow others to concoct for them an enemy that does not exist.

It was also a call to action for Muslims to go out of our comfort zone and explain who we are. I am certain that this can bring huge dividends in terms of recognition and respect for us. We can defeat the few haters who have inordinately loud voices, through coalition building with friends from the faith communities and like minded organizations, fighting together for justice and values that we all believe in. That was the message that we heard loud and clear from the healing and hope that came about through pro-active cooperation on the 10th anniversary of the tragedy that bruised all of us so much.

Chapter 19

Recognized by the Supreme Court

I have often wondered what would happen if the 'Open House' events had been covered by the media. I called several of them on many occasions and got excuses ranging from "not newsworthy" to "we don't have a person available at this time" to "this is interesting"...but we hardly ever heard back from them.

Fortunately there were some in the media that were sensitive to covering the Muslim narrative. Susan Campbell, a journalist at the *Hartford Courant,* is one of them and has been a steadfast voice of reason and understood our efforts at outreach. She has often been criticized for doing her job. Susan has become a good friend of our family as she has gotten to know that we are far from the kind of people we have been vilified to be.

We realized that while doing all of what we were doing we also had to have events where the public would be able to come and hear about who we are and ask any questions that they may have. This was the fourth area that the Muslim Coalition of Connecticut had earmarked as areas that needed addressing. The 'Taste of

Ramadan' and the 'Footsteps of Abraham' programs were meant to do exactly that.

For the 'Taste of Ramadan' we chose the towns of Newington, Glastonbury and West Hartford, all suburbs of Hartford, and sent invitations to adjoining places of worship to join us for an evening of conversation. Our theme was fasting, as Ramadan is the month of fasting for Muslims. We had a Jewish, Christian, and Muslim speaker give an account of fasting from their own faith traditions and we allocated most of the time for table conversation. The discussion ended at sunset when we broke our fast and shared a meal with our guests. They thus had an opportunity to witness the sunset prayer, one of our five daily congregational prayers and partake in a hearty meal together. We were also achieving the two things that the prophet commanded us to do on migrating to an area – spread peace and feed people.

Those who came were very supportive and asked us to continue our outreach. They promised to bring more people when they came the next year, and many did.

The 'Footsteps of Abraham', another 'open house' centered on explaining the Islamic pilgrimage, the Hajj, which is the fifth pillar of Islam (see Appendix for details). We held this event in Glastonbury and West Hartford and so involved communities regularly, maintaining the dialogue as we educated people about our faith. Non-Muslims usually do not realize that Hajj, is a once in a lifetime pilgrimage for Muslims, and celebrates the life and example of the prophet, messenger and patriarch Abraham. So we invited Christian and Jewish clergy to give their perspectives on Abraham and on pilgrimages sacred to their tradition, as we explained ours.

The 'Taste of Ramadan' and 'Footsteps of Abraham' evenings became powerful events which have always been packed successes.

As our open houses became well attended, the model started being followed by Muslim student organizations in fast-a-thons, where non-Muslim students are encouraged to fast with the Muslim students one day during Ramadan and break their fast all together with an educational program on Islam and fasting. They also organized 'Islam Awareness Week' in universities throughout the state – education was the key. Many non-Muslim university female students began to wear the hijab (the head cover worn by Muslim women) for a day to show solidarity with female Muslim students. Muslim students invited scholars to lecture on different aspects of Islam during the Islam Awareness Week.

Gradually, students on university campuses learned more about Islam. Muslim chaplains, almost all of them trained at the Hartford Seminary and therefore adept at dialogue techniques, were particularly helpful. We had outstanding pioneering chaplains who are now working at universities throughout the nation with these models of dialogue. Abdullah Antepli, who was at Wesleyan University in Connecticut is now at Duke University in North Carolina, Sohaib Sultan, who was at Trinity College in Connecticut is now at Princeton University in New Jersey, Omer Bajwa who is the chaplain at Yale University in Connecticut, and Bilal Ansari who was a prison chaplain and then went on to Williams College in Massachusetts is now at Zaytuna College, the first degree awarding Muslim Liberal Arts College based in California. These were some of the amazing young men who have really left a positive impact in Connecticut and there have been many male and female Muslim chaplains who have followed in their footsteps.

We also began to have more interfaith discussions and broke bread more often with faith leaders, in particular those who had reached out to us. We had this outreach at many interfaith banquets that were organized by MCCT.

MCCT members were called upon to help organize and lead the Islamic Circle of North America's (ICNA) annual interfaith banquet, held in Hartford, Connecticut. We coordinated ICNA's interfaith banquet for as long as ICNA held its annual conference in Hartford, which was for seven years. ICNA's annual conference attracts over ten thousand people and was held at the Connecticut Convention Center. For the interfaith banquet we invited about a hundred and fifty guests. We invited faith leaders to speak on specific topics - one speaker from each Abrahamic faith community, and after the speeches we had an extended amount of time reserved for table discussions.

The topics covered included:
    a. family as the center of religious life,
    b. universal healthcare,
    c. religious intolerance,
    d. preparation for the tenth anniversary of 9/11.

As more leaders began to take the message of reconciliation to their communities, more invited us to participate in dialogue with them.

We also began to proactively participate in issues that were important to our nation. One such issue was universal health care and our involvement resulted in our getting to know activists in the health-care debate.

In 2005, I spoke at the Legislative Building at the State Capital in Hartford, Connecticut, on the need for universal health care to be addressed at the state level. This was before the Federal government's Affordable Care Act (Obamacare). It was unconscionable to me as a physician, to know that 1 in 6 people in this nation did not have health coverage. Although this is still a work in progress, it has been taken up at a national level and there is real progress on it.

The need for universal health care became the theme of one of our leadership banquets. We highlighted the Islamic emphasis on healing and helping the needy. We gave awards to some outstanding people actively involved in 'Sustinet', that was supposed to be the state sponsored program for universal healthcare.

Governor Lowell Weicker, the former governor of Connecticut, gave a great keynote speech on the need for universal healthcare, which he called a human right. It was a breakthrough, as he was a former Republican turned Independent, and in general the Republican Party opposed moves to establish universal healthcare.

In the process of working on universal healthcare we also worked with many Hispanic and African American inner city leaders and developed a very cordial relationship with many of them.

We also developed a relationship with Christopher Donovan, the Speaker of the House in the State of Connecticut. Not only did he help us with our banquet on universal healthcare, but also on the issue of domestic violence awareness and environmental stewardship. We made domestic violence awareness and environmental stewardship the theme topics of other banquets. All of these events, although not clearly open houses, served the same purpose. People got to know us and learned what the Qur'an and the *Sunnah* (the teachings and example of Prophet Muhammad) had instructed us on, with regard to helping the poor and standing in solidarity for social justice issues.

We wanted to work with law enforcement as they were the first responders, meaning that in a crisis they were the first to respond, once the emergency services are activated. They needed a true account of who we are and not a second hand account of what to fear about us. I worked with, and got to know Deputy Chief Neil Dryfe, of the Hartford Police Departments, who went on to become the Chief of Police in the Cheshire Police Department. He is one of the nicest people I have met. He realizes that good policing means that the community needs to trust their law enforcement community, and he worked to that end. It was important to integrate but not lose our identity as American Muslims, which is a tough balance that all immigrant communities struggle with, especially when it comes to giving the next generation a positive identity as Americans, while maintaining a healthy heritage of the past.

Chief Dryfe arranged for me to make a presentation at the Greater Hartford Police Chiefs meeting, and also arranged for me to be involved in cadet training on cultural awareness, all of which happened around 2005. Through all of this, we were allowing for law enforcement to get to know us directly. The police were very grateful and we were glad to be doing this training pro bono. It was a win-win.

We also invited the FBI outreach person, Ron Offutt, to a Muslim leadership meeting and asked him to speak to us about what the FBI was doing to help the Muslim community, and tell us how we could help in the nation's security. Ron arranged that we organize a training session for federal as well as local law enforcement agents, which we did, again pro bono.

The Muslim community made presentations on Islam, our demographics, our beliefs and our goals as a community. It was rather sparsely attended as it was a voluntary opportunity, but many who came clearly wanted to help in this relationship building opportunity.

Before he was transferred to another part of the country, Mr. Offutt often expressed his frustration at not being able to do certain things as restrictive orders came from above. For example, the local chapter of the Muslim community civil rights group, the Council on American Islamic Relations, CAIR, wanted to participate in the training session. It only made sense as they represented the Muslim community. But members of CAIR, which was classified as an 'unindicted co-conspirator' by the Federal government, were not allowed into the FBI building to give a talk. Ron Offutt was very apologetic and, by changing the venue from FBI headquarters to a Middletown facility, he found a way to proceed with CAIR on board.

We had difficulty doing an outreach and sensitivity training workshop pro bono, when speakers from groups vilifying us were being paid and could talk unhindered and attendance was often compulsory (see next chapter). It did not make a lot of sense.

We needed to acknowledge and build on our relations with law enforcement, and in November 2012 our annual banquet was themed "Working together for Safer Neighborhoods". We gave awards to Police Chief Neil Dryfe from Cheshire for his work when he was deputy chief of Hartford Police Department, and also to John Olsen, President of the AFLCIO, the latter, for his willingness to work with us on the healing event on the 10th anniversary of 9/11. The Governor of Connecticut, Dannel Malloy was the chief guest, and speaker of the House Chris Donovan also attended. There were two tables of police chiefs and their families, a table of judges and their families, and about three hundred and fifty other attendees.

I was the chair of this banquet, and the keynote speech was by the chaplain at Princeton University, Sohaib Sultan, whom I had asked to speak about 'Demystifying *Shariah*', and he did a phenomenal job.

After the event, one of the judges came up to me and said, "Today I have been educated and if ever there is any anti-*Shariah* legislation that comes across my desk, I will throw it out". After this event many police chiefs have also reached out to us and asked us to provide education on Islam. The banquets were achieving their objective of spurring on dialogue and we needed every opportunity to do that.

As a result of the banquet we were also invited to participate at the Police Academy training class in Hartford in 2012, and to speak at the Southern and Western Police Chiefs' meetings that year as well. All of this was humanizing us to law enforcement, who would now think twice when they heard or received a hate mailing about Muslims that kept making the rounds on the internet.

On Law Day 2013 we received a huge honor in recognition of all the outreach we were doing. In spite of the atmosphere of Islamophobia and legislation against *Shariah* in other states, the Supreme Court of Connecticut gave the Muslim Coalition of Connecticut its Law Day award. The Supreme Court letter to the President of MCCT reads that we were being recognized "...due to the education and outreach that the Muslim Coalition of Connecticut is providing". It speaks volumes about the open mindedness of those responsible in the highest court of this state, especially when compared with many other states that were considering hate legislation against us.

Aida, the president of MCCT, as part of her outreach had spoken to the judicial branch employees about Islam and had made a huge impression on them. It played a big role in helping them understand Islam and was a major factor in helping us attain this award. We now realized that the Supreme Court Justices were aware that our organization was striving to change the narrative in the most positive and American of ways, through education and outreach.

Chapter 20

Understanding the Hate Radicalizing Our Youth

We struggled to understand how, despite all we were doing, the published statistics showed that the number of U.S. citizens who had a negative impression of Islam kept rising; 17% in 2001, 40% by 2010 and more than 50% in 2015. This was mirrored in all media reports. The fear was emanating from an organized source and that source was difficult to discern and the media kept propagating it. More difficult to discern was the purpose of this vilification of us. Mass e-mailings played their role; one accused us of "waiting like wolves for the opportunity to suddenly attack Americans." There were others that accused us of much worse. They were all just scaring people who did not know us into fear.

The reality is that there were people like myself, 1 in 10 of all U.S. physicians (despite being only 1% of the population), who try every day, often desperately, to cure people of fatal illnesses, regardless of their backgrounds. There are other Muslims in small businesses trying to revive the economy and there are accountants, lawyers, and computer technologists working to keep industry in the U.S. vibrant.

As President Obama has reminded us, there are sports figures from Mohammad Ali to Shaquille O'Neal to Kareem Abdul Jabbar and Hakeem Olajuwon, bringing great fame to our nation in the sports arena, all of who are Muslim. There are still other American Muslims fighting patriotically for this nation in its armed forces. Muslims have fought in the Revolutionary war, the Civil War and in 2011 there were three thousand five hundred serving in the US armed forces. The American Muslim community is a healthy mix of professionals, very comfortable with our American Muslim identity and happy to be in a country where we truly have the religious freedom many countries we came from do not, despite, in some cases being Muslim majority countries. Personally, I would not choose any other country to make my home.

When putting together 'open houses' and other events to get to know each other, we had not expected the quick positive responses from those we had hoped to make our friends, and to get their admission that we were not as the media portrayed us. But we also did not expect the strength of deep racial and religious prejudice among some and that the fear and hate would be moving faster than we could counter, despite our outreach and education.

Our false sense of security and ignorance of what we began to call Islamophobia came to an abrupt halt with the publication of Fear Inc[24]. Only after this publication did we realize the names of those involved and their modus operandi in sowing the hate against

---

[24] https://www.americanprogress.org/issues/religion/report/2011/08/26/10165/fear-inc/

us and how Islamophobia had become a big business with lots of money to earn. A very unpatriotic big business!

As we looked into it seriously, we found fortunes were being made from peddling prejudice against us. When such people found they were welcomed by law enforcement communities and at Congressional hearings, they doubled down, making little effort to back up their stories with facts or to conceal their lies.

Following a six-month long investigative research project, the Center for American Progress released a 130-page report which reveals that more than $42 million (to 2011) from seven foundations over the past decade have helped fan the flames of anti-Muslim hate in America. The authors — Wajahat Ali, Eli Clifton, Matt Duss, Lee Fang, Scott Keyes, and Faiz Shakir — worked to expose the Islamophobia network in depth, name the major players, connect the dots, and trace the genesis of anti-Muslim propaganda.

The report, titled "Fear Inc.: The Roots Of the Islamophobia Network In America," lifts the veil behind the hate, follows the money, and identifies the names of foundations who have given money, how much they have given, and who they have given to: Donors Capital Fund $20.8 million, Richard Scaife foundations $7.9 million, Lynde and Harry Bradley Foundation $5.4 million, Rusell Berrie Foundation $3.1 million, Anchorage Charitable Fund and William Rosenwald Family Fund $2.8 million, Fairbook Foundation $1.5 million, Newton and Rochelle Becker Foundation $1.1 million

The money has flowed into the hands of five key "experts" and "scholars" who comprise the central nervous system of anti-Muslim propaganda:

Frank Gaffney, David Yerushalmi, Daniel Pipes, Robert Spencer, and Steven Emerson.

Money poured into their coffers, as million dollar right-wing corporations and non-profit organizations mistakenly believed that what these phony-pundits were selling was related to national security.

Most disturbing was the fact that the government was paying these 'experts' to spread their hate and insecurities to law enforcement and intelligence agencies.

General Martin Dempsey, the chairman of the Joint Chiefs of Staff, was reported to have ordered a top down review of training after students questioned some of material taught in a class called 'Perspectives on Islam and Islamic Radicalism', which was taught to mid-level officers at the Joint Forces Staff College in Norfolk, Virginia; as reported in the *New York Times* of April 25th 2012[26].

Captain John Kirby, a pentagon spokesman, has agreed "There are some unprofessional things being taught to students in professional military education curriculum".

Captain Kirby went on to add, "Military trainers and guest lecturers appeared to be advocating ideas and beliefs and actions that are contrary to our national policy. ...and disrespectful of the Islamic religion"

That article went on to say, "The pentagon asked for this review a year ago as there were similar complaints about the FBI

---

[25] http://thinkprogress.org/politics/2011/08/26/304306/islamophobia-network/
[26] http://www.nytimes.com/2012/04/26/us/new-review-ordered-on-anti-islamic-themes-in-military-courses.html

training on counter terrorism". The Pentagon was concerned about the FBI training, when in 2010 the FBI had Robert Spencer, (co-founder of 'Stop Islamization of America') speak to the 'Tidewater Joint Terrorism Task Force', spreading similar hate.

Are we being unfair to ask for a speedy review of military and intelligence training? Robert Spencer ranks as one of 'The Dirty Dozen' Islamophobes by the independent national media watch group *Fairness and Accuracy in Reporting (FAIR)*[27]. It classified these dozen as those who systematically "spread fear, bigotry and disinformation".

His organization's name "Stop Islamization of America" should have been enough of a tip to his agenda. The litmus test should be whether that epithet "Stop ...ization of America" would be fair to be attached to any minority group trying to live peacefully as the vast majority of American Muslims are doing.

Irrational fear, spread by these hate filled people, on a substrate of lack of knowledge of Islam, often leads to hate which can very quickly descend into hate crimes. Wouldn't it be better to identify and address those who suffer from Islamophobia and who spread the fear/hate, than to allow them to spread their fear and anger? In 2010 there was a spike in hate crimes, as I recounted earlier, almost certainly related to all the hate speech around the Park 51 fear mongering by Pamela Geller, Robert Spencer's partner in "Stop Islamization of America".

---

[27] http://fair.org/article/the-dirty-dozen/

The counter argument by those who spread hate is always, "our constitution gives us the right to free speech". My assertion is that media has the responsibility to avoid highlighting what hate-mongers say if it is clearly going to cause more fear and hate that often directly leads to violence, as we have seen now repeatedly. There are some, including *Fox News,* that have a voracious appetite for highlighting what the hate mongers say and interviewing them ad nauseum. That is why there are two present *Fox News* personalities on 'The Dirty Dozen' by *Fairness and Accuracy in Reporting,* both Sean Hannity and Bill O'Reilly win that accolade. If you listen to them, you quickly understand why.

But there is little action taken to stop the hate. Many in law enforcement and intelligence are doing a tremendous job, while many other law enforcement leaders are turning a blind eye to this hatred being spewed.

Meanwhile, we as Muslims want someone to deal with our serious concerns so we can contribute as much as we can to the country we have chosen and love. We can't do that if we are, with increasing frequency, being portrayed as the enemy. The effect this is having on our youth is even more concerning. Our youth are being bullied with subtle insinuations of terrorism, and that is making them feel isolated, while sinister on-line extremist groups invite them to a false utopia where they could proudly live as Muslims without any Islamophobia; under ISIS. American Muslims can least afford our youth to get attracted to these social media hate groups, and nor can America and that is why we are speaking out.

To politicians and some in the media, I say, please be responsible and stop being used to spread hate. You are only serving the goals of the terrorists when you drive a wedge between American Muslims who love this nation and our neighbors.

People being exposed to this hatred went to their representatives, often at the request of these Islamophobes, demanding that something be done about "this Muslim menace." Most recently we heard it at a Donald Trump rally in the presidential election cycle of 2015/16. As Donald Trump did not correct this person and instead encouraged this scapegoating based on fear, many other lawmakers did the same.

Laws get passed based on these fears. With those laws we are moving away from that freedom loving nation to an insular and insecure nation that our founders would hardly recognize.

As I am an American citizen and a Muslim, I have decided to expose some of these individuals who were not only inventing the fear and hate they spread, but don't care for the consequences of their actions. In doing so, I should also reveal the now-confirmed lies they invented about Islam to do so.

Steven Emerson

Self described 'Terrorism "expert"' Steven Emerson, with his Investigative Project on Terrorism (IPT) is consumed by hatred of Islam.

This is the same man who said that the Oklahoma City bombings had all the "hallmarks of a Middle Eastern terrorist attack", which later turned out was carried out by a Christian who was not from the Middle East. At best, he is ignorant, at the worst, he is a dangerous man capable of spreading fear while pretending to care about our nation's security. I believe he is the latter.

Emerson is quick to generalize and stereotype and once he gets an audience to listen, he is very difficult to neutralize. Even after he is proven wrong a trail of fear remains.

He produced a documentary 'Jihad in America' which paints the American Muslim community with a broad negative brush and raises funds for his projects by telling donors they were "in imminent danger from Muslims"[28]. Those funds he then used for his own ends. He has transferred $3.3 million dollars, according to Wikipedia, that he raised for his non-profit IPT to his for-profit SAE productions, where he is the sole employee!

Ken Berger, president of *Charity Navigator* (a nonprofit watchdog group) has explained why this is wrong: "Basically, you have a nonprofit acting as a front organization, and all that money going to a for-profit...it's wrong. This is off the charts." (Wikipedia)

Emerson has testified, unhindered, before Congressional committees and spoken at law enforcement and intelligence establishment seminars, always reiterating that Muslims are dangerous. Like most fanatics, if anyone disagrees with him, he calls that person dangerous. He suggested that Governor Chris

---

[28] http://en.wikipedia.org/wiki/Steven_Emerson

Christie is also a 'problem' because he has defended Muslims. What Governor Christie has actually done is to refuse to propagate the myth that Islam is a religion of hate.

Emerson said the reason Christie is dangerous is, "...because he has sided with Islamist forces against those who worry about safeguarding American security and civilization." Notice how Emerson plays the national security card to spread fear. We would see this repeated often!

On May 1, 2012, Emerson and Daniel Pipes (discussed below) co-wrote an article defaming Governor Christie in *National Review*. Their sum-up final paragraph reads:

> In short, Christie has hugged a terrorist-organization member, abridged free-speech rights, scorned concern over Islamization, and opposed law-enforcement counterterrorism efforts. Whenever an issue touching on Islam arises, Christie takes the Islamist side against those — the DHS, state senators, the NYPD, even the ACLU — who worry about lawful Islamism eroding the fabric of American life.

The same day, Matt Duss a foreign policy analyst and a contributing writer for the *Prospect*, reprinted the whole article and responded:

> 'A perusal of the authors' case against Christie reveals it as comically weak, full of highly questionable characterizations and buttressed by links that don't actually demonstrate what they're supposed to.

According to '*RightWeb*', a website that tracks militarists who try to influence U.S. foreign policy, Emerson has been repeatedly criticized for producing faulty analyses and having a distinctly anti-

Islamic agenda, yet he is a frequent guest on news channels including *Fox News*[29]!

He is the same person who claimed, on *Fox News*, that Birmingham, England, is a Muslim only city that non-Muslims are not allowed into, during an interview in January 2015. The *YouTube* clip that shows this, betrays the agenda and ignorance of the *Fox News* interviewer, Judge Jeanine Pirro, in a typical *Fox News* type interview where she aids Emerson in his false claims by egging him on[30].

The British Prime Minister, on hearing about this, called Emerson a "complete idiot" but this is the caliber of interviews that spreads fear, ignorance and hatred of Muslims, and needs to be called out. It is this type of falsehood that makes our youth feel a sense of betrayal by the media and promotes this notion of 'us versus them'. Although Emerson 'apologized', Prime Minister Cameron said "But what he should do is look at Birmingham and see what a fantastic example it is; bringing people together of different faiths and different backgrounds and building a world-class brilliant city with a great and strong economy." Emerson is blind to that side of peaceful co-existence. It is in fact what drives the anger that fuels his hatred.

Daniel Pipes

Daniel Pipes is founder and director of the 'Middle East Forum' and 'Campus Watch', organizations that focus and attack any

---

[29] http://rightweb.irc-online.org/profile/Emerson_Steven
[30] https://www.youtube.com/watch?v=-_zF7nbEvwY

scholar who is critical of Israel. He, like Emerson, depends on getting support for his ideas by building fear of those who oppose him. Campus Watch "blacklists" academics who are critical of Israel. To protect Israel, he advocates that a watch be kept on Muslims in government, Muslims in their places of worship and basically Muslims everywhere in his misguided attempt to protect Israel.

Pipes is one of those also criticizing President Obama for hiding the fact that he is a Muslim, which shows you how extreme he is! Despite all this, he has been given credibility by the media and is repeatedly invited to speak.

James Zogby, an Arab American and founder and president of the Arab American Institute (AAI), has criticized Pipes for having an "Obsessive hatred of all things Muslim".

Pipes has raised funds for Geert Wilders of the Netherlands, the extreme right wing politician who wants to prevent Muslim immigration to Europe! Pipes has defended the WWII internment of Japanese, and said at an American Jewish Congress convention in 2001:

> "I worry very much from a Jewish point of view, that the presence and increased stature and affluence and enfranchisement of American Muslims...that it will present true dangers to American Jews"[31].

A problem with some who are extreme Zionists is that they feel that part of protecting Israel is to attack all Muslims.

---

[31] http://www.islamophobia.org/news.php?readmore=132

As soon as the public begins to realize speakers like Emerson and Pipes are irrational and the ranting of the irrational is not trustworthy, it seems that a new person replaces them.

Walid Shoebat

Walid Shoebat, an evangelical Christian, also took the centerfield in the hate Islam game. He claimed to have been a Muslim fighter for the Palestinian cause who suddenly 'saw the light' and became a crusader for Christianity.

Shoebat's 'fantastic' story has been uncovered on CNN as being totally false[32]. *The Jerusalem Post* has also disputed it.

Naturally, Muslims are concerned when people like Shoebat are still believed, particularly when law enforcement and intelligence communities invite him to speak, despite having all the tools through the PATRIOT Act to verify who tells the truth and who does not. Why they are unable to do what a reporter from CNN, Anderson Cooper, did when he found out that Shoebat, who is now a fervent supporter of Israel, concocted his past, is quite beyond belief!

Shoebat advocates monitoring Muslim student groups and mosques, in fact, when you listen to his clips, he really advocates monitoring all American Muslims. It was through this being uncovered that we learned why student associations, mosques and religious communities were being monitored by the NYPD – in a

---

[32] http://www.youtube.com/watch?v=pJNO0dBhZVk

total waste of tax-payer money. Freedom, to these extremists, means a Police State spying on everyone they don't like.

Isn't this what the early American settlers fled from Europe to avoid? We now understood why the NYPD went on wild-goose chase spying expeditions on Muslim students in the Tristate area (New York, New Jersey and Connecticut), when intelligence officers are required to listen to lectures by people like Shoebat.

Robert Spencer

Robert Spencer is one of the anti-Muslim inner circle according to the Southern Poverty Law Center (SPLC). SPLC suggests his influence is far greater than himself because of the right wing media support of him.

Spencer runs a website called 'Jihad Watch' and with Pamela Geller co-founded the organization 'Stop Islamization of America'. Spencer wants moderate Muslims to denounce part of the Qur'an, his litmus test of their moderateness.

I don't know any Muslims who would want to fulfill his definition of moderateness, especially when his misperception of Islam and the Qur'an is obvious. His extremism is exposed by his misquotes and misinterpretations of authentic texts, often quoting sources out of context.

Karen Armstrong, who was a Catholic nun, has written books on many religions. She has criticized Spencer's books, and he has written many, in his zeal to milk this cash cow for all it is worth.

She calls his books "a gift to extremists who can use it to prove...that the West is incurably hostile to their faith".

What she is saying is that it is this sort of person who perpetuates the war against the west by people who believe that America is at war with Islam. This, despite our government's efforts to do the opposite, thus he puts our troops and government representatives at risk everywhere in the world.

I don't think this kind of person even cares for the collateral damage to our troops who are being killed sacrificing their lives for this nation, as long as he is able to get his hateful message out there and make lots of money doing that, which he has. I often wonder how people like Spencer sleep at night.

Pamela Geller

Pamela Geller, Spencer's partner in hate, is co-founder of 'Stop Islamization of America'. They are ideologically a perfect couple. Most of what she advocates is the same as Robert Spencer, spreading fear about "creeping *Shariah*" to her rhetoric on Jihadists.

She wrote in Arutz Sheva:

"It galls me that the Jews I fight for are self-destructive, suicidal even. Here in America, Israel's real friends are in the Republican Party and yet over 80% of American Jews are Democrats. I don't get it. The conventional wisdom on the Left is that Israel is an oppressor and her actions are worse than the world's most depraved and dangerous regimes. Chomsky, Finkelstein, Soros – these men are the killers." Wikipedia

The vast majority of Jews reject her hate in the name of Judaism, as most Muslims reject the extremism of Muslims in our name. She encourages Israel "to stand loud and proud and give up nothing". By not giving up an inch, extremists also perpetuate conflict without an end and are never the solution, and that is not their objective.

Geller has said she believes that the Muslim terrorists are practicing pure Islam, thus making all Muslims the enemy. She has also claimed that Hitler was inspired by Islam. Facts it seems do not stand in the way of her hatred. *Russia Today* in an excellent interview exposed her hatred and asked her why she had a picture of the prophet Muhammad with a pig's head on her blog if she was not an instigator of hate[33].

She has been a constant opponent of mosques in America, especially the Park 51 cultural center, which she calls the "mega mosque on ground zero", even though it is neither on ground zero nor a mosque.

Her tell all advertisement on public buses defines her motive "In any war between the civilized man and the savage. Support the civilized man. Support Israel, defeat Jihad". Her rant on public transportation in many cities in the United States defines the extreme fear she lives with for the misguided love of Israel.

David Yerushalmi

---

[33] http://www.youtube.com/watch?v=HzPTkFTx98E&feature=related

The New York Times exposed this lawyer from Brooklyn, David Yerushalmi for spreading fear around *Shariah*[34]. Yerushalmi, a Hasidic Jewish lawyer, drafted model legislation casting *Shariah* as one of the greatest threats to American freedom since the Cold War.

In the atmosphere of heightened awareness after 9/11, Yerushalmi's message caught on, but as the *New York Times* suggested his fears were more imagined than real.

Muslim leaders are not asking for *Shariah* in America, because American laws allow us the freedom to practice our religion without hindrance. Yerushalmi's is a reactionary piece of legislation and it sends an alarmist message, and creates hysteria. The *New York Times* pointed out that religious law, whether Islamic or Jewish, is mainly used in divorce and custody proceedings or in commercial litigation. In the United States it has been used only about 50 times in the last 3 decades, they pointed out. Therefore, the point was not to address a true legal concern but to create mass hysteria and fear, and from the reaction of the spread of this legislation he has achieved his nefarious goal.

Yerushalmi started work when he was in Israel and lived in a large settlement in the Occupied West Bank - an illegal settlement according to all American governments to date and according to international law. That is likely where he was influenced in his hatred. Interestingly, his legal clients include Pamela Geller, in her fight against Park51, and many other Islamophobes.

---

[34] http://www.nytimes.com/2011/07/31/us/31shariah.html?pagewanted=all

On Yerushalmi's website, he has proposed making observing *Shariah* law a felony punishable by 20 years in prison. That means that if we follow *Shariah* guidelines and pray five times a day, or give in charity, we should be put in jail! That is literally what he is saying, because that is what *Shariah* is - guidelines to live a spiritually fulfilling life. (See Appendix section for clarification about *Shariah*).

Shariah is similar in many ways to Jewish *Halachic* law and that is what is most ironic! He has joined with Frank Gaffney, another Islamophobe, but with connections in the neo-conservative world, and now an advisor to Ted Cruz, to get his message across the country. Mr. Gaffney has financed him with hundreds of thousands of dollars and they used the Tea Party to push this legislation in different states.

Both Catholic and Jewish groups which would be negatively impacted by his hate legislation have opposed Yerushalmi. To date over twenty states have considered these laws and according to the Washington Post, Oklahoma, Florida, Georgia, Indiana, New Jersey and Minnesota have rejected the call as of 2012[35].

Muslims are amazed at how many people these days go around saying "no *Shariah* law" without knowing the first thing about *Shariah* and that it is not even 'law'. We understand that this opposition is principally around the way '*Shariah*' is portrayed in the media, where they show a suicide bombing or a stoning to death in an Afghan village while talking about *Shariah* law. Subliminal

---

[35] http://www.washingtonpost.com/national/on-faith/anti-shariah-bill-defeated-in-oklahoma-senate/2012/04/06/gIQA6NxB0S_story.html

messages completely confusing their viewers as to what *Shariah* is and spending no time clarifying it with any scholarly input.

If you watched the Republican presidential debates of 2011/2012 you would have seen each of them pledge never to allow *Shariah* law in America. I am certain that none of them knew the first thing about *Shariah*, particularly, that there is no such thing as '*Shariah* Law' to begin with.

Muslims have become more and more concerned that the Republican Party has recently pandered to those who are spreading hate, particularly through the "Tea Party". It is sad, as Muslims share many of the religious and family values of Christians and Jews that the Republican Party claims to represent. In its present hateful form, Muslims would be hard pressed to vote Republican, just as immigrants and all minorities do.

Frank Gaffney

Frank Gaffney is President of the American Center for Security Policy. He was part of the Bush administration and now part of 'team Cruz'. According to Republican strategist Grover Norquist, he is described as having "racial prejudice, religious bigotry [and] ethnic hatred" against Muslims.

He has been linked by some to the biased training of the military and CIA for which, as I have illustrated, General Dempsey is doing a top down investigation of the training due to the amount of hate that is being taught by some of the instructors.

Gaffney, is also involved in the Obama non-citizen conspiracy story, and has been known to fabricate other such stories and run with them. His Center for Security Policy, founded in 1988, also gives negative information to representatives like Michele Bachman and Louie Gohmert, who became experts in giving vicious anti-Muslim tirades, including against Secretary Clinton's deputy chief of staff Huma Mahmood Abedin, who happens to be a Muslim. They call such appointments, the "infiltration of government by Muslims". Note the similarities to McCarthy.

The Southern Poverty law center not surprisingly named Gaffney the anti-Muslim movement's most paranoid propagandist.

In 2010, Gaffney together with Lt. Gen. William Boykin and several others, including Yarushalmi, wrote a book "Shariah: The Threat to America". When such high-ranking military officials are openly willing to be associated with such paranoid thinkers, it becomes extremely concerning. Gaffney testified in Murfreesboro, Tennessee at a hearing for a proposed mosque that "Islam is a threat to America and, therefore, the mosque is a threat!"

He has accused our celebrated Gen. David Petraeus, of "submission to Shariah" for condemning the Qur'an burning by Pastor Terry Jones! General Petraeus meanwhile was trying to protect our troops who have to face the backlash from this evil act.

Can we have such paranoid extremists as advisors to the president of our beloved United States of America? Unfortunately from all we hear, Ted Cruz seems an extremist himself, as evidenced by all the hate for Islam he espouses.

There are many others, including Brigitte Gabriel, founder of 'American Congress for Truth' ACT - a featured hate group by the Southern Poverty Law Center. She has been similarly exposed for the hatred she has for Islam and the falsehood she spreads. There is just not enough room in this book to cover all the hateful individuals. Suffice it to say this is an extremely unpatriotic industry that brings out the worst in humanity, through our worst prejudices. They often use national security as a reason for spreading their fear and you will notice many of the organizations these people head, having national security as a prominent alibi.

Chapter 21

Spasms of Hate – Roots of Radicalization

It has become a sad but true fact that beginning two years prior to any presidential election, when the election season begins, starts a cycle of hate fuelled by opportunistic politicians that use fear to scapegoat someone or something and so prop up their national security credentials.

Since 9/11 this has been all about driving their credentials of strength at the expense of Muslims. I would have expected opportunistic politicians to do well in countries that had a poorly educated population but this phenomenon has become dangerously divisive in America and gets worse with each election cycle.

Some modern day politicians base their positions on issues to take advantage of poll swings. Their moral and ethical compass seems to depend on the direction of the wind, rather than staking positions of integrity. Even so, to stigmatize and scapegoat a minority to keep your job is particularly despicable.

That is why some in the Republican Party have lost so much credibility recently. They have abandoned most demographic groups in this nation to pander to the fear of the extreme right. What they don't realize is that they are actually destroying their chances of becoming President by losing those who now see them as extremists – which is the majority of Americans.

This is not guesswork; I can illustrate this from the Muslim community. Only 8% of Muslims are registered Republicans today but according to CAIR, 78 % of Muslims voted Republican in 2000. In 2012, over 85% of Muslim Americans voted for Barack Obama – that was a much higher percentage vote than came in from any other faith community. It is a remarkable swing that happened because the Republican candidates have outdone each other in pandering to and fostering fear and hate to portray themselves as strong in national security terms. But bullying, which let's face it picking on minorities is, is a sign of insecurity and real weakness.

If the Republican Party wants to be taken seriously by the American Muslim population and other minorities, it will need to correct its fear based politicking very quickly.

In a *Pew Study* poll in 2011, 69% of Muslims say that religion is an important part of their daily lives. Muslims know that many of our religious values are no different from Christian and Jewish values. The Republican Party could have a much greater influence if it could shed its hateful side and claim these values based voters. Every time 'Islam' is said in an insulting and derogatory manner however, we notice who said it and remember that when we vote.

With the conspiracy theory accusing Barack Obama of being a closet Muslim, we felt that anger was also being directed at the

Muslim community. Let me walk you through a few of the last few election cycle fear based politics, so you understand this better.

Conspiracy theories are given a louder than normal voice in talk radio and *Fox News* as they interview those who have these weird theories frequently, especially around the time of the elections. This has led to the population becoming unnecessarily scared, as can be seen in a comment and John McCain's response during a presidential campaign rally back in 2008, when a woman asked him, regarding Obama "Isn't he an Arab?"

McCain replied: "No he is not an Arab, he is a good man!" Yes, he really said that. The not so subtle insinuation is that Arabs are the bad people.

It was General Colin Powell who protested the fact that McCain's was also a very racist statement, as it portrays Arabs as bad, and Collin Powell went on to ask, "Are we saying it is wrong for a Muslim to be a President of the United States?". At that time that statement was abhorrent, not so any more.

In the 2012 presidential campaign the spasm of hate was fuelled by still more racist and bigoted statements. Consider Herman Cain who was at one point the Republican front-runner against Obama. He said he would require Muslims in his cabinet to show proof of loyalty to the Constitution to serve in his administration and also said he would not do that to a Catholic or Mormon. After noticing his poll numbers improve with those statements, he then swore not to appoint a Muslim to his cabinet at all. Newt Gingrich went even lower comparing Islam to Nazism[36]. Hard to believe but yes these really did happen.

I believe that these candidates are aware of the fact that this is against the Constitution and everything it stands for, but have actively decided to ignore that and promote this fear, as they see their poll numbers rise immediately, as more extremists support them. Their integrity up for sale based on polls. Unfortunately, with each election cycle we experience more xenophobic statements from some elected officials and the whole nation seems to get more radicalized by this hate.

The hate rhetoric has real consequences and, in 2012, directly as a result of the hateful rhetoric, more than ten years after 9/11, we were seeing the most number of mosques being vandalized and burned in America. This illustrates a direct correlation between fear mongering during the campaigns and the hate crimes that result.

How do we stop the hateful rhetoric and extremist following?

I cling onto the belief that when Americans understand the nature of the fear based campaigns and that they are being used by politicians they will dismiss these politicians. I trust that this beautiful nation and its enlightened Constitution cannot allow this breed of hatred to win out. I have, however, been told by many Jews that that is what their parents told them about Germany and what happened in the 1930's and 40's. "An educated people would not vote for hatred based on fear". We need to have an enlightened

[36] http://america.aljazeera.com/opinions/2015/4/american-muslims-should-fight-islamophobia-in-2016-elections.html

dialogue on hate and respect for the diversity of religions in America. After all this is a true first amendment issue.

It was one of the major reasons I decided to write this book. We cannot afford to keep quiet. If I highlight some of the problems and clarify some of what we as Muslims are doing to counter the fear, and generate some discourse around this, perhaps I could prevent some very dangerous fanatics, both Muslim and non-Muslim, from destroying the delicate fabric of tolerance and good will in America.

In a rally we organized against Islamophobia in 2010, to address the growing hate, Rabbi Eric Silver of Temple Beth David in Cheshire, Connecticut, showed that he understood the dangerous path the country was taking when he said: "Germany was primed for a while before 'Kristallnacht' through a media campaign, through hate groups and then a party of hate and a leader of hate, in Hitler, before the holocaust happened". He was alluding to the fact that we should have a zero tolerance policy for scapegoating and vilifying minorities in any way, before it leads to worse.

I became driven by the knowledge that we had to learn the lessons of history before the same mistakes destroy our country as it had the nation I was born in, Sri Lanka, during the Civil War there. We have to find the soul of our nation again. Anti-Semitism and Islamophobia should have no place in this or any society. The problem is once you release this genie of bigotry and xenophobia out, it takes a life of its own and it is very difficult to put the genie back in the bottle.

Hard to believe but in 2015 the presidential campaign rallies of the Republican candidates got even nastier, in terms of their bigotry, and the hate crimes and violent incidents against mosques hit an even higher peak. Right in our back yard in Meriden, Connecticut, a mosque was shot at, in response to the heightened rhetoric, after the Paris shooting incident. The perpetrator, a former Marine explained that after drinking too much he had committed this criminal act but explained "As a neighbor, I did have fears, but fear is always when you don't know something. The unknown is what you are always afraid of. I wish I had come knocked on your door, and if I spent five minutes with you, it would have made all the difference in the world. And I didn't do that."

Dr. Ben Carson, a Neurosurgeon, quickly realized the value of scapegoating and stigmatizing Muslims. His first comment about no Muslim being allowed to be president brought him both popularity and money and he and his campaign cynically even referenced that in continuing his Muslim bashing bigotry.

George Pataki, another Republican candidate for president clarified this irony best when he said that in the past they said an African American could not be president. How ironic is it now that an African American says that of another minority!

Governor Bobby Jindall and Senator Ted Cruz, likewise, have made horribly xenophobic statements about Islam and Muslims in their attempts to show strength and to boost their national security credentials and appeal. Jindall and Cruz do this by trying to woo the Evangelical extremist vote, but they destroy our national unity through that.

As we get to the final two, Cruz and Trump, let's analyze for a minute their rhetoric. As Cruz wins more primaries, he has noted how popular Muslim bashing is, and has adopted a variant of it for himself. There is an extremist flavor in Cruz's vitriol and his choice of advisers that maybe even more problematic than Donald Trump's.

Cruz wants law enforcement "to patrol and secure Muslim neighborhoods." Isn't that the worst in profiling? When questioned about it, he actually congratulated Mayor Bloomberg for the NYPD spying, even though it was found to be ineffective and counterproductive and had to be abandoned. Mayor de Blasio called Cruz's comments "reprehensible", clarifying that "it is not about safety and security – it is demagoguery". The mayor went on to explain that there are over nine hundred Muslim officers in the NYPD. NYPD Commissioner Bratton, after predicting that Cruz would not become the president, said in regard to his comments "he does not respect the values that represent this country", calling his comments out of line.

Trump however trumps them all in trumpeting xenophobia throughout the country. In his campaign he became a specialist on insulting and denigrating minorities. He started off with Hispanic Americans of Mexican origin and moved on quickly to attacking Muslims, a much easier target to bully and get away with. He advocates having a special database of Muslims, having surveillance of us, shutting down some of our mosques and making Muslims wear special identity cards or badges. What more can he demand to look more like Germany in the 30's?

As he realized his poll numbers going up with each nasty statement he made, he doubled down, lying confidently about "thousands upon thousands of Arab Muslims celebrating in New Jersey after 9/11", without a shred of evidence to prove that. Even after he was conclusively proven to be lying, he continued repeating his false claims. He often refers to us as "those people", thus making 'us' the 'them' in this 'us versus them' portrayal.

As his poll numbers kept going up he used that to actually explain the need to continue his bigotry saying it was popular! How opportunistic and without moral scruples can you be, if your campaign is based on taking advantage of the negative portrayals and stereotyping of minorities. But for him it worked and so he quickly went on to the most unimaginable, he would ban Muslims from coming to America.

I would not be so concerned if I did not think this fear based politics works, the sad fact is it does work. Sri Lanka suffered a twenty five year civil war that killed over one hundred thousand people because of politicians using religion and ethnicity to further their individualistic goals.

If elected president, and I still very much doubt that the American people would ever do something so ridiculous, he would be a most arrogant leader that would set us back immensely in our struggles to coexist peacefully within America and throughout the world. We can see a prelude of this almost daily with the violence at his rallies. Our standing in the world would be irreparably damaged. In his campaign he has insulted Chinese, Mexicans, Arabs, Muslims, Blacks, Russians, people with disabilities, women and the list goes on. The only demographic group spared is his own.

This is the Grand Old Party started by Abraham Lincoln, the author of the Emancipation Proclamation which was the first real step against the racism of slavery. Hard to believe how far they have gone in the wrong direction.

This present irrational fear has to be contrasted with our nation's founding and the respect that Islam and its prophet were given.

If you go to the Supreme Court building of the United States of America, there is a frieze of a portrayal of Prophet Muhammad holding the Qur'an signifying his position as an upholder of justice[37]. Our founding fathers respected and recognized Islam and Islamic Law.

Similarly, on the dome of the Library of Congress, there is recognition of Islam as having contributed significantly to the civilization of the world[38].

Our country did not just survive, it became the undisputed leader of the world due to the embrace, recognition and respect it

---

[37] http://zombietime.com/mohammed_image_archive/misc_mo/
[38] http://myloc.gov/ExhibitSpaces/MainReadingRoom/TheDome/Pages/default.aspx?Enlarge=true&ImageId=3a238
842-fc7f-4e20-980e-2cfde671a488%3A7dc4057f-df0d-48d3-a97b-
e9af72c8f47d%3A31&PersistentId=2%3A3a238842-fc7f-4e20-980e-
2cfde671a488&ReturnUrl=%2FExhibitSpaces%2FMainReadingRoom%2FTheDome

paid to the contributions of other great civilizations and religions. Our Founding Fathers had the courage to do so.

Our greatest enemy in this nation is not the manic few who are so insecure that they see themselves threatened by something or someone all the time. Our greatest enemy is those who let other people's fears become theirs and give into the prejudices of those few.

I look back to a better time when America guided the rest of the world through its confidence and its focus on our unity, encouraged by our diversity. "United we stand and divided we fall", made famous by John Dickinson in his revolutionary Liberty Song in July 1768 symbolized that. Patrick Henry, one of our founding fathers and a governor of Virginia in a speech in 1799 said, "Let us trust God, and our better judgment to set us right hereafter. United we stand, divided we fall. Let us not split into factions which must destroy that union upon which our existence hangs."

It is worth thinking of the wisdom in such words which have been quoted for generations with a purpose.

Chapter 22

The Europe We Fled

The original Pilgrims came to America from England after the Church of England separated from Catholicism and forced its population to join the Church of England. Some under William Bradford fled this forced conversion to establish the first colony in Plymouth in 1620. Since then, waves of immigrants came to America fleeing religious persecution across Europe and from the rest of the world, more recently, seeking a better life away from the chaos and dictatorships. The United States is still regarded as the beacon of light that the statue of liberty welcomes them to.

The Constitution and Bill of Rights were written by our founding fathers, acutely aware of the harmful effects of religious zealotry and intolerance. Our nation was born to be tolerant and avoid the extremists from ever forcing religion on others in this new nation.

But that Europe we fled has suddenly become an example for some in America, on how we should marginalize another community, in this case Muslims. This intolerance in Europe has resulted in catastrophic consequences with regard to its minorities, whether they were Jewish, particularly in the 1930's and 40's, or Muslims at the present time. These are the 'Muslim only cities' the extremists, like Steven Emerson, are talking about. They are the ghettoized minorities that are not enfranchised or made to feel welcome.

As they marginalize and ghettoize minorities, their youth are joining more extreme groups like ISIS, who offer them an Islamic utopia – at least on social media. Do we really want to learn lessons from the same continent our founding fathers created laws to differentiate us from, especially their religious persecution of minorities? In order to analyze what is going on in Europe you have to understand the demographics of the people involved.

There are three groups of European Muslims:

- The first group comprise of the professionals that migrated for employment and opportunity and are generally doing well. They are well adjusted with their lives in Europe and comfortable in their faith.

- The second group came as manual labor from all over the world, a byproduct of the colonialist past of many of the European countries. They reside in inner cities and struggle to make ends meet, but are there legally. They struggle the way the inner city folk in America struggle.

- The third group came because of the difficult situation in their home countries. These immigrants and refugees are mainly from Africa, Asia and, more recently, parts of the Middle East and are struggling in Europe, because of their legally unclassified status and because they reside in the inner cities.

In the US we have the same demographic groups but the people in these demographics are different. The majority of Muslims are from the first group, here as professionals and generally doing well. They are working as doctors, engineers, computer technologists, accountants and active in the small business community. The inner city does have Muslims but in America, the inner city population is largely non-Muslim. They are largely African-American and Latino.

Illegal immigration is a problem in the US as well but the demographic group is different, it is mainly from Latin America and come here due to financial and other difficulties in their countries of birth.

These differences are due to our geographic location and our non-colonialist past. For those who say "look at Europe, it is what America will become", they are either very ignorant of this demographic difference or deliberately want to mislead people to propagate fear.

One problem in many European countries is that many inner city populations are not enfranchised, valued or incorporated. From them we can learn what not to do to our inner cities in America. The solution to the inner city problems is not bigotry and scapegoating, as has happened in France in the past, but enfranchisement and supportive care. In the US we are doing a better job at this than in parts of Europe, although we have a long way to go.

The LA riots of 1992 are similar to the Paris riots of 2005. In Paris, however, the rioters were mostly Muslims and in LA they were mostly African-American. France has not dealt as well as California in assimilating its minorities, especially under Presidents Chirac and Sarkozy. The inner city issues there are getting worse, and the rioters are blamed for the problems they face. Instead of dealing with them in a positive way, the government decided to make the Muslim community the scapegoats, declaring that Muslim women who wore the headscarf were not assimilating. So, instead of addressing the real problems of housing and the ghettoization of these inner city residents, the headscarf was banned.

The rhetoric Muslims face in Europe is the same rhetoric that Mexican and Central American immigrants face in the US. Although in Europe the inner city folk happen to be majority Muslim, the problem has nothing to do with their religion but rather with the geography and socioeconomic status of people, that must be addressed with foresight and clear vision by their governments.

European countries also have many laws that do not show tolerance or respect for diversity. Two examples of this are the banning of the head-scarf in French public places in 2004 and the banning of minarets in Switzerland in 2009. In France this was after a bill was passed in the senate 276 to 20, and in Switzerland it was after a referendum on banning minarets. These laws stigmatize

Muslims directly and unnecessarily make them feel isolated and alienated.

In the United States, where there is much more maturity about these issues, this type of law would be deemed unconstitutional and challenged in the Court system, as is being done with the wave of 'anti-*Shariah* law' legislation. We have much more faith in the American system of judicial oversight, checks and balances and our Constitution and Amendments. Until Europe learns to tolerate diversity the way the United States has learned, there will be conflict between different cultures, which may go on for decades to come. At least that, it seems, is what the extremist groups in Europe seem to want and certainly the terror groups like ISIS and Al-Qaeda want as well. This is a recipe prepared by the extremists on all sides to make sure we are hating and fighting each other forever. But we, the moderate voice, are the majority and we can change that narrative

Europe is still struggling from the intolerance of extremism and fascism, whether one is referring to the fascist leaning groups headed by Geert Wilders, the far right Dutch politician, or Marine Le Pen, the far right French National Front candidate who ran for President in France, or for that matter the English Defense League, a far right hate group that is working against Muslims and immigrants in the UK.

What is concerning is that in America the hate individuals mentioned, for example Daniel Pipes has supported Geert Wilders and Pamela Geller has spoken positively about the English Defense

League. In fact Britain banned Pamela Geller from coming to the United Kingdom due to her extremist views, but she is free to hate in the U.S.A.

Chapter 23

Jewish/Muslim Relations

It is vital that we realize the historic healthy relations between the Muslim and Jewish communities. Most Muslims understand the suffering that Jews in the diaspora suffered even before the Holocaust.

Professor David J Wasserstein, the Eugene Greener Jr. Professor of Jewish Studies at Vanderbilt University explains that Islam had saved Jewry centuries ago, after the Muslims became the rulers of the previous Persian Empire, where most of the Jews lived.

"Jews were not confined to ghettos, either literally or in terms of economic activity. The societies of Islam were, in effect, open societies. In religious terms too Jews enjoyed virtually full freedom." [39]

Wasserstein points out, however, that Jews and Christians were on opposite sides during the pre-Islamic period when the Roman Empire converted to Christianity. The majority of Jews lived in the Persian Empire, which included ancient Babylonia, where the Talmud came into being. The Roman Empire became largely

---

[39] http://www.thejc.com/comment-and-debate/comment/68082/so-what-did-muslims-do-jews

Christian, partly due to forced conversions to Christianity, which included the Jews of that time, explains Wasserstein.

Within a hundred years of Prophet Muhammad's death, almost the entire Jewish population was under Muslim rule – from North Africa and the Middle East to parts of Iran and Syria.

"This new situation transformed Jewish existence. Their fortunes changed in legal, demographic, social, religious, political, geographical, economic, linguistic and cultural terms - all for the better," wrote Wasserstein.

Jews were given citizenship and there were no restrictions to the practice of their faith.

"The Jews of the Islamic world developed an entirely new culture... Instead of being concerned primarily with religion, the new Jewish culture of the Islamic world, like that of its neighbors, mixed the religious and the secular to a high degree. The contrast, both with the past and with medieval Christian Europe, was enormous.

Much of the great Hebrew poetry, written since the Bible, comes from this period - Sa'adya Gaon, Solomon Ibn Gabirol, Ibn Ezra (Moses and Abraham), Maimonides, Yehuda Halevi, Yehudah al-Harizi, Samuel ha-Nagid, are only some of the poets well known today who belong in the first rank of Jewish literature."

"Where did these Jews produce these works? When did they and their neighbors achieve this symbiosis - this mode of living together? They did it in centers of creativity and learning. The most outstanding was Islamic Spain, where there was a true Jewish

Golden Age, alongside a wave of cultural achievement from the Muslim population. In Islamic Spain - waves of Jewish cultural prosperity paralleled waves of cultural prosperity among the Muslims and exemplified a larger pattern in Arab Islam. In Baghdad between the ninth and the twelfth centuries, in Kayrouan (in Tunisia) between the ninth and the eleventh centuries, in Cairo, Egypt, between the tenth and the twelfth centuries; the rise and fall of cultural centers of Islam was reflected in the rise and fall of Jewish cultural activity in the same locations."

The Jewish diaspora in Europe, were out of the Islam's influence, and suffered greatly. They were expelled from several countries, including England by King Edward I in 1290 in an edict that lasted 350 years.

Other times were worse, such as the Spanish Inquisition of 1478, followed in 1492 by the expulsion and forced conversion of Jews by Ferdinand and Isabella, the Catholic rulers who defeated the Islamic Andalusian Empire. In 1492, the Alhambra Decree (also known as the Edict of Expulsion) caused Jews to be expelled from Spain, some parts of Portugal and Italy.

Most of the Jews travelled with the Muslims and were given refuge in Muslim lands from Morocco to the Ottoman Empire. In France, there were waves of expulsion of Jews, particularly in the 12th to 14th century, in Ukraine in the 1600's and the Russian pogroms in the late 1800's to 1900's.

In Europe, the culmination of hostility against the Jews was, of course, the Nazi Holocaust. Today, many Jews and most

Americans do not know of this history and the historical proof that Jews thrived under Islamic rule.

I have noticed our local Jewish community is at the forefront of human rights issues. Rabbis want to work with the Muslim community and to defend us against Islamophobia. My good friend, Elizabeth Aaronsohn, a retired professor and daughter of a Rabbi, spoke at an interfaith gathering the Muslim community had organized. She explained that her father spoke strongly about justice and that she believes it her duty to do the same.

She fought for black civil rights in this country as many other Jews did, and even got arrested for doing so. She changed her Passover Seder to a Freedom Seder because, she explains "I realized I can't be free until all my brothers and sisters are free." She feels her brothers and sisters are all humanity, not just those of her own faith.

The title of her talk that day was, "Justice, Justice Shalt Thou Do." She told us about the prophetic Jewish tradition that her father taught her and the responsibility this brought. Her talk reminded me of the Qur'anic injunction regarding justice:

> **"O believers! Stand out firmly for justice, as witnesses to God, even against yourselves, your parents, your kin and whether it be against rich or poor; for God can best protect both. Follow not your desires, lest you swerve and if you distort or decline to be just know that God is well acquainted with what you do" Q 4:135**

The trauma suffered by the Jewish community historically is undeniable. As one of my Jewish friends explained: "After centuries of suffering in the Diaspora, we finally have a homeland in Israel and with all the suffering we have gone through, the pogroms and the Holocaust, we feel a need to support that state. It is a communal sense of anxiety for the future of our people due to the repeated trauma we have undergone".

In January 2016 I travelled to Spain and visited Al-Andalusia and the cities where Jews thrived under Islamic rule, in fact they were the most prosperous Jews in the world under Islam. Their fate changed very rapidly under the Spanish Catholics, with anti-Jewish riots in 1392 and then their expulsion in 1492. Between those years the Jews suffered terribly. They were ghettoized and treated in the most horrible way and many were forced to convert to Catholicism.

It is vitally important that as Muslims we acknowledge that Jews suffered horribly in the Diaspora and not make light of or deny the trauma that the Jews suffered or deny the Holocaust.

But, after getting this homeland, and particularly after occupying more territory in 1967, Israel's policies have not reflected the Jewish values of justice and tolerance, especially for the occupied Palestinians. How can it ignore the Palestinian suffering in the occupied territories, the anxiety of a people dispossessed, traumatized and yearning for a homeland of their own, just as they themselves once did?

Those non-Jewish people in the West Bank, both Christian and Muslim, have lived in a state of limbo since 1967, that is for almost fifty years. They have, during that time, been without a voice, without a vote, with road-blocks and check-points, under the constant harassment by settlers, who burn their olive trees and acquire Palestinian property through illegal land grabs for settlements, sometimes even poisoning the water supply to chase away the Palestinian owners of this land.

These are not just my views and words but the views and words of international observers. One voice of reason is Jewish scholar Peter Beinart who in his book "The Crisis of Zionism" explains this well.

The illegally built settlements, in the words of President Carter, have resulted in a state of apartheid in these occupied lands. It is the same message delivered in 2007 by another Nobel Peace Prize winner, Bishop Desmond Tutu in Boston, when he spoke at a conference urging Israel "to deal with the oppressed, the weak, the despised compassionately, caringly, remembering what happened to you in Egypt and much more recently in Germany" [40].

He compared the Palestinian suffering in the occupied territories to that of the South Africans under apartheid. The late president Nelson Mandela, the first black president of South Africa, said much the same.

Working with representatives of the large American Jewish organizations I found challenging because of their widespread support for Israel "no matter what". They continue to do so, even when Israel has the most extreme policies of the most right wing Israeli government in history, which this Netanyahu government seems to be. That is a problem for all of us.

---

[40] http://jewishvoiceforpeace.org/content/waging-peace-archbishop-desmond-tutu-delivers-sabeel-conference-keynote

I was fascinated that in his book, Professor Beinhart explains the problems we are facing. "The American Jewish organizations' approach of supporting the most right wing Likud government positions on Israel and lobbying for these means they were immediately at loggerheads with the American Muslim community." Beinart explains that these large organizations are also at loggerheads with a large majority of the Jewish American community. The majority of Jews and Muslims in America want a fair settlement to the Israeli-Palestinian problem.

Professor Beinhart illustrates that the occupied areas are disobeying the very declaration of the state of Israel itself, which promises "complete equality of social and political rights to all its inhabitants irrespective of religion". He says, "Unless American Jews end the occupation that desecrates Israel's founding ideals, Zionism will become a movement that fails the test of Jewish power". He also explains how American Jewish organizations from the American Jewish Congress to AIPAC (American Israel Public Affairs Committee) to the ADL (Anti Defamation League) all support the Israeli government approach of settlement building, which is illegal, and opposed by the US government. If the Palestinians are not given a state, Beinart writes, this will ultimately result in one of two things: a single, apartheid state, as is happening in the occupied territories now, or a state, that if it gives all people their rights, would be suicidal for Zionism, as the Palestinian population will be larger than the Israeli population.

He also acknowledged that all the Arab countries have offered to make peace with Israel if it ends the occupation. If Israel wants peace – the ball is in its court. I have not heard this narrative explained so well by a Jewish scholar and I illustrate it here because it explains our dilemma with the major Jewish organizations.

How does this affect us as American Muslims?

In its quest to legitimize the pro-Israeli position, the major American Jewish organizations have had to stifle efforts to discuss the subject openly. The increased vocalizing of these concerns for the occupied people, not just from the Muslim community but by prominent internationally recognized figures like Bishop Desmond Tutu, the late President Nelson Mandela and President Jimmy Carter and now many young Jewish activists, including J-street and Jewish Voice for Peace, and many more human rights minded Americans has caused alarm in these traditional Jewish organizations.

The majority of Jews, according to Peter Beinart, are much more liberal than the organizations that represent them. He illustrates this by looking at their voting record and their support for President Obama, who has been an advocate for ending settlement building and working on peace. All Israeli governments, through their subsidies to people who live in occupied settlements, have encouraged illegal settlements in the occupied lands, supporting a schizophrenic position of on the one hand stating their support for peace and on the other hand destroying any chance of peace.

We have had fruitful and healthy discussions of our similarities with many synagogue communities, rabbis, and congregants, but when it comes to the major American-Jewish organizations we have struggled. There is a tension between us that prevents meaningful discourse and their opposition to Islamophobia has sometimes been tepid and sometimes verging on toleration or even acceptance of it, as in the ADL position regarding the Park 51 issue. This resulted in renowned journalist Fareed Zakaria returning the award that the ADL had given to him, writing:

> "Given the position that they (the ADL) have taken on a core issue of religious freedom in America, I cannot in good conscience keep that award. So, this week, I am going to return to the ADL, the handsome medal and the generous honorarium that came with it. I hope this might spur them to see that they have made a mistake and to return to their historic robust defense of freedom of religion in America, something they have subscribed to for decades and which I honor them for."[41]

Many people, including rabbis, e-mailed and called me to say that the ADL's position did not reflect their Jewish position, which further illustrates this dichotomy that Professor Beinhart refers to. He cites a Gallup poll showing that American Jews were the religious group most likely to say that American Muslims face widespread discrimination.

---

[41] http://www.huffingtonpost.com/2010/08/06/fareed-zakaria-returns-an_n_674099.html

AIPAC, the lobby group that advocates pro-Israel policies to Congress and the President, on the other hand, has hosted some Islamophobes, including Steven Emerson at their annual convention, making us even more concerned.

I must very clearly point out that in America, Jews and Muslims are natural allies. We are both minorities and have a lot in common religiously. We must overcome our differences and work together. Pointing out the challenges we face is a call for reasoned dialogue but dialogue we must. The alternative to dialogue is always worse.

Chapter 24

The Extremist Challenge

"O believers! Stand out firmly for justice, as witnesses to God, even against yourselves, your parents, your kin and whether it be against rich or poor; for God can best protect both. Follow not your desires, lest you swerve and if you distort or decline to be just know that God is well acquainted with what you do" Quran 4:135

I would be remiss if I did not start this chapter by criticizing the extremists in my own faith community. From the above verse of the Qur'an, that is exactly where God starts as well. Be witnesses against yourselves, first, in standing up against injustice.

In criticizing extremists within the Muslim community, the obvious example of an extremist group is the "so called Islamic State", as President Obama has referred to them as, and I concur. For a group to call itself Islamic and carry out the most barbaric and horrendous acts that they do is frankly anti Islamic.

From a historical perspective, Islamic State is a relatively recent phenomenon. It is a terrorist group that began in Iraq and was known as 'Al-Qaeda in Iraq', and formed after our invasion of Iraq. Al-Qaeda in Iraq began as a national resistance movement against the U.S. occupation and the Iraqi government, that was Shia dominated. When Sadam Hussein, a Sunni leader was deposed, his army, which were largely Sunni led, were dismissed by the Coalition Authority and joined Al-Qaeda in Iraq, at least covertly, supporting the subversive activities against the Shia led government and the U.S. administration in Iraq.

When Syria destabilized, the Shia leader of Syria, Bashar Al-Asad, started getting assistance from Shia led Iran, Iraq and Hezbollah and so the Sunni resistance in Iraq joined with extreme elements of the Syrian resistance to Bashar and formed the Islamic State of Iraq and Syria (ISIS). This has resulted in a civil war in both Iraq and Syria pulling the surrounding countries, as well as the superpowers into the mix, creating a proxy war between America and Russia, between Sunni and Shia and extremists on all sides.

It is a mess!

The largest number of people being killed, in fact, is Muslim. I would go so far to call it genocide against Muslims.

To attribute this horrible civil war to Islam is to be very ignorant of the facts. They are armies of a political/sectarian struggle and would love to have the legitimacy of religion, but we cannot afford to give them that. Ironically, president Obama has stood strong against doing that, but it has been the Republican extremists like Ted Cruz and Donald Trump, in order to delegitimize all of Islam, that have been yearning to give IS the legitimacy of "Islamic". Constantly using the phrase "Islamic Terrorists" and, in fact, taunting the President for failing to give IS that legitimacy!

Cruz and Trump are in the 'Clash of Civilization' camp that believes that somehow Islam and Muslims aren't good enough to have the values The West has, including democracy, freedom and liberty. Therefore "stop the immigration of Muslims, stop the process of integration of Muslims, we have to reverse course". That is what they are saying. How far do we reverse course? Do we reverse course until the Spanish Inquisition or the Crusades? Do we really want to go back to that? This is a very convoluted time and not to understand all the dynamics playing out can be quite confusing and misleading. However, this election is also crucial in that it could lead to a leader that maybe regarded as an extremist and therefore it behooves us to understand what is at stake.

As for the actions of the Islamic State and its leadership, they have been declared 'against Islam' in scholarly works by Muslim leaders from across the globe[42]. I advise you to go to the website lettertobaghdadi.com (Baghdadi being the leader of IS) and see the whole scholarly dissertation against the actions of these extremists from an Islamic perspective. This is once again to show you that Muslims from across the globe are very critical of extremists within our faith and very forthright about it, but we have no way, in this destabilized part of the world, to prevail against them. Nevertheless, we are still strongly opposed to their actions, despite what the media keep telling you about the moderate voice being quiet in the face of these criminal acts of terror.

---

[42] http://www.lettertobaghdadi.com/14/english-v14.pdf

We have to also acknowledge extremism in other faith communities. The Connecticut Council for Inter-Religious Understanding (CCIU) is an organization representing members from nine religions. There is a healthy discussion and criticism of nations that oppress their minorities. If all agree a letter is generated from CCIU critical of the nations that oppress their minorities and publicized on the website of CCIU. It takes courage to be able to criticize nation states of your own faith that don't treat their minorities fairly, but that is the criteria that God demands when he speaks about justice. The Muslim board members of CCIU signed on to letters criticizing the treatment of Bahai's in Iran and Copts by the government of President Morsi of Egypt. Freedom of religion is one of the principles of *Shariah* and therefore they must be allowed to practice their faith without oppression.

However, during the Gaza war (2008-9) when most unbiased media condemned the inordinate force used against the Gazans by the Israeli government and the huge number of civilians killed, criticism of Israel in the form of a letter, was immediately followed by threats of resignation from the Jewish Federation representative. It is irrational to be completely blind to the injustices of your own people. This extremism devoid of justice does not lead to a just society. Justice seeking Jews, including presidential candidate Bernie Sanders, have vocalized the inordinate force used against Gaza and the extraordinary number of civilians killed, refusing to go to the AIPAC conference and support extremism. It is not anti-

Semitism to criticize a nation that occupies and does not give rights to its minorities.

Nobody is justifying the terror acts of Hamas, but we must be able to criticize extreme policies by a government that perpetuates a conflict unnecessarily, increasing the suffering and displacement.

The majority of Jews are much more rational and want a more just position vis-à-vis Israel. Peter Beinhart in his book 'The Crisis of Zionism' states that in the late 1990's almost two thirds of American Jews supported establishing a Palestinian state and a large majority supported halting settlement growth in the occupied territories. In 2005, three out of four American Jews supported U.S. pressure on both Israel and the Palestinians if it would help bring peace. Unfortunately these Jewish voices are not represented in the large Jewish organizations. The organizations tend to muzzle the discussion and dissent and that is what happened at CCIU.

Most Jews don't want their religion, and the nation representing their religion, to be associated with the occupation of another people and the awful human rights conditions of these occupied Palestinians.

The Israeli government at present, under Prime Minister Netanyahu, is very hawkish (extremist), and is supported by the very hawkish (extremist) American Israel Public Affairs Committee (AIPAC), that has a huge influence on policy matters leading to deadlock in U.S. influence in the Middle East. The lobbying groups have an inordinate effect on the politics of this nation, particularly in Congress at present, and together with the Evangelical lobby we are likely doomed to more of the same policies and deadlock in peace negotiations for awhile. Their paralyzing effect on American Foreign Policy has rendered the U.S. unable to be a fair moderator in this conflict. Even the suggestion of fair moderation, by none other than Donald Trump, was criticized by the others, especially Cruz, for days. This lobby influence has been well illustrated by Professors Mearsheimer and Walt, from the University of Chicago and Harvard University respectively, in their book *'The Israeli Lobby and U.S. Foreign Policy'*.

Where the United States could have a hugely positive effect in solving this most vexing problem, through the effect of lobby groups, the conflict has been allowed to fester and America's standing has been allowed to be downgraded the world over. Furthermore, in my opinion, any injustice gives power to the extremes and it is certainly one of the factors playing a role in the destabilization of the Middle East. Seeing the Palestinian suffering is a thorn in the side of most justice seeking people throughout the world.

Yes Israel is an ally of the United States but we cannot allow injustice to go unopposed. As Rev. Dr. Martin Luther King Jr, said "Injustice anywhere is a threat to justice everywhere."

To his credit, the President has tried repeatedly to get the peace process, beneficial to all, up and running. Prime Minister Netanyahu, on the other hand, has been able to stand firm against President Obama, with the support of the lobby groups and their influence on Congress. When there was obvious tension between our President and Netanyahu over settlements in particular, Netanyahu would go to Congress and get repeated standing ovations, weakening the hand of the president. This is problematic for obvious reasons. Netanyahu's direct interference in the Iranian-US negotiations was treacherous, but there is not enough said about this extremist and his extremism.

What is even more concerning for Muslims is Netanyahu's constant use of the term "Islamic terror" as an excuse to continue the illegal occupation and segregation policies of his extreme government. In fact there is a vocal minority of Christian Palestinians who are active in their opposition and resistance to the occupation. For obvious reasons Netanyahu never refers to this Christian resistance as "Christian terror" for fear of alienating the evangelical right wing support he gets in America.

Where the major American Jewish organizations are a concern, the far bigger concern was that several extreme Zionists were actually leading the hate and Islamophobia. Pamela Geller was one of the worst. Her belief was that in order to legitimize the existence of Israel, she has to delegitimize the existence of the Muslims in America. You will find this in most extremists from all faiths – they try to delegitimize 'the other'.

In one of her seething presentations in a synagogue in Long Island, on a candidate's forum on the State of Israel, she spoke about President Obama speaking to the *Jihadist "Ummah"* (community – in Arabic). She loves using Arabic terms that nobody in her audience knows and then she will give it the most horrific

217

translations. She explained how Israel is the bastion of hope and of how the people of Gaza don't have an issue with starvation, they have an obesity problem and how Gaza was teeming with swimming pools and malls! Anybody who knows anything about Gaza knows that after repeated Israeli bombardments what is left is mostly in ruins. They don't even have building materials to rebuild their houses as Israel blocks building materials from coming into Gaza. Truth never stands in the way of extremists like Pamela Geller.

Our concern of course is that when you have such vitriolic hate mongers speaking in synagogues you misguide the whole community into fear and ignorance. Her organization's billboard campaign explains her bigoted logic: "In any war between civilized man and the savage, support the civilized man - support Israel, defeat *Jihad*!" These advertisements have been put on the public transport network in several cities.

Daniel Pipes, another extremist, has done the same through trying to delegitimize the American Muslim presence admitting "I worry very much from a Jewish point of view, that the presence and increased stature and affluence and enfranchisement of American Muslims...that it will present true dangers to American Jews"[43]. Perhaps what he means to say is that the presence of American Muslims will affect his and his ally's extreme pro-Zionist position, which I tend to agree with. Through his organization 'Campus Watch' he even promotes surveillance of scholars in the U.S. that are critical of Israel!

---

[43] http://www.obsessionforhate.com/thepundits.php

Steven Emerson has also been concocting stories critical of Islam and Muslims for decades and is now on the fundraising team for pro-Israeli American Jewish organizations. Emerson views all Muslims as a threat and paints all Muslims in the most bigoted way. "Emerson's prime goal", according to the Wall Street Journal is "to whitewash Israeli governments and revile their critics." AIPAC has had him at their annual conference which is concerning for Muslims, but not atypical for AIPAC, which promotes the most extreme positions on Israel. As *Mondoweis*, an internet based independent news network put it, "AIPAC has put its seal of approval on Islamophobia... The appearance of a major fomenter of Islamophobia at AIPAC is a prominent example of how mainstream Israel lobby groups legitimize Islamophobia." What is surprising is that most politicians, especially those running for president, go to AIPAC's annual conference despite this extremism. Bernie Sanders has been the outlier in refusing to go to their convention, despite being Jewish, I salute him for that integrity and honesty.

David Yerushalmi, who is known for bringing forward anti-*Shariah* hysteria through legislation banning *Shariah* in America, also comes from an extreme pro-Israel position. In an article Philip Weiss explains his extremism as coming from a hatred for the Palestinians[44]. Yerushalmi has written in the past, according to Weiss, that "One must admit readily that the radical liberal Jew is a fact of the West and a destructive one." Therefore he rejects the

---

[44] http://mondoweiss.net/2011/08/in-long-piece-on-yerushalmis-anti-shariah-campaign-nyt-cant-talk-about-his-contempt-for-a-murderous-non-people-palestinians.html

values based Jewish identity, the prophetic model of Judaism, for the ethnocentric nationalist Israeli identity.

Another example of this portrayal of all Muslims as the problem is the controversial film which the NYPD officers were made to watch, the "Third Jihad", which Muslims view as hate indoctrination. This is a video produced by the Clarion Fund, a pro-Israel New York City based nonprofit organization, founded by an Israeli-Canadian citizen Raphael Shore. His other movie is "Obsession: Radical Islam's war against the West". DVD's of his movies were distributed free in battleground states, to elicit as much fear of Muslims and President Obama prior to the 2012 elections.

These extremists often couch their hatred by portraying themselves as fighting "radical" or "extremist" Islam, but when you view these movies or listen to them speak you get the impression that America is at war with Islam and that is clearly their intent.

Why is our law enforcement leadership allowing this message to corrupt the training of police officers? When NYPD police officers were made to watch the movie the "Third Jihad", the officers regarded the movie as "ridiculously one sided and inappropriate", in interviews conducted with them[45]. The movie looks at the most extreme countries and paints Islam through morphing those images with the American Muslim community and what America will look like "under" Islam. Remember all along that Muslims are around

---

[45] http://www.huffingtonpost.com/2012/01/24/nypd-training-included-video-the-third-jihad_n_1227889.html

1% of the U.S. population and the U.S. is not at risk of being "taken over" by this small Muslims minority!

For American Muslims, our acceptance and peaceful co-existence depends on being portrayed correctly. If we cannot diagnose all the elements of the problem, we are not going to find solutions. The American Muslim community is eager to change the narrative of Muslims presented as "being the problem", when we are in fact working towards developing a healthy environment and to make our homeland safer and better. We want to do that with pride and self-confidence in our identity as Muslims just as Catholics, Jews and other minorities in America are proud of their heritage and their country.

While we are less affected by the large "extremist" evangelical challenge in New England, from among them come a lot of misperceptions about Islam as well.

Brian McLaren, in the article "My Take: It's Time for Islamophobic Evangelicals to Choose", writes about being brought up an evangelical and receiving "pious sounding, alarm bell ringing" hate e-mails about the evils of Islam from his own relatives, most of them complete fabrications about the religion[46].

He points to the fact that many of these evangelicals do not have any Muslim friends and many are prejudiced by so called "Christian" television and radio broadcasts. This media highlights many Islamophobes who lie, including Walid Shoebat, who are hosted by evangelical talk radio and TV broadcasters such as Janet

---

[46] http://religion.blogs.cnn.com/2012/09/15/my-take-its-time-for-islamophobic-evangelicals-to-choose/comment-page-5/

Parshall and John Hagee. He further highlights the problem of Christian bookstores that have books by Paul Sperry for example with titles like 'Infiltration: How Muslim Spies and Subversives Have Penetrated Washington'.

None of this is conducive to peaceful co-existence and none of it, I suggest, is in keeping with the teachings of Jesus or Moses, just as none of the Islamic extremism is in keeping with the teachings of Prophet Muhammad.

Elected representatives, such as Michele Bachmann and Louie Gohmert, end up so influenced by this hateful rhetoric that they start accusing good American Muslims such as Huma Abedin, a senior aid to Secretary Clinton, of being an infiltrator and affiliated with the Muslim Brotherhood. In this case, a good and patriotic American is being vilified and accused of being an infiltrator simply because she professes to practice Islam.

You can see from this that the methods of vilifying and stereotyping ordinary Muslims by some extremists will result in all of us being dragged into a never-ending conflict.

This book is written as a call to sanity. Extremists are sown from the same cloth and we must reject their ideology of hate completely. Until we all take the higher path and reject all forms of extremism we, as a nation and as a global village, will suffer the consequences that we are seeing all too often. These extremists must not be used by immoral politicians for their own petty political ends or by slanted media to support their flagging ratings. We are one nation under God. The moderate voice must stand up and speak out against extremism in all its forms, everywhere.

Chapter 25

Charting Our Future – Beyond the Golden Door

When I began to write this book, in the Spring of 2012, I wanted it to be a book looking forward and so I considered calling it 'A Thousand Open Houses', for all the opportunities we got to get to know each other. This however did not adequately capture the substance of the book. I therefore changed the title to 'Stigmatized: from 9/11 to Trump and beyond – An American Muslim journey', as it reflects the unfair stigmatization of the Muslim community in America since 9/11, that has only gotten worse with time. I described our experiences, as a Muslim community, to better illustrate the challenges we faced and are facing along this journey and our attempt to always respond in the most positive of ways.

Although American Muslims wish there had been no 9/11, no pain to our fellow countrymen and women, no associated hijacking of our religion by the extremists, and no reverse extremism (Islamophobia) in our nation and our fragile and interconnected world. The fact is, our beautiful religion, our great nation, and this global village, are all affected by extremism of different forms but sown from the same cloth of intolerance. With modern media highlighting the acts of extremists and with social media transmitting information at ever increasing speeds, our challenges to maintain our fragile balance have become increasingly important.

Historically, we have seen extremism spiral out of control before civil wars, genocides and world wars, and they are usually fanned by prejudice and bigotry. We must actively choose to take the higher road that leads to understanding one another with respect for our differences, than the road leading to the former.

The beautiful verse of the Qur'an I quoted before, says it all:

"O mankind! We created you from a single pair of a male and a female and made you into nations and tribes so that you may know each other. Verily the most honored of you in the sight of God, is the most righteous among you and God is full of knowledge and well acquainted with all things." Qur'an 49:13

In Islam, God created us all from one couple, Adam and Eve. After He created Adam, He breathed of His divine breath into Adam, giving us the divine attributes to be able to overcome our base self that even the angels worried would "create mischief and shed blood", according to the Qur'an.

All of us have to face challenges. We must assess whether we are going to allow ourselves to be used by those troubled people who have to have an enemy to make them feel relevant. We can crumble and become their victims or turn to the basic teachings of our role models and divinely guided messengers whether that is Moses, Jesus or Muhammad and stand strong on our values.

I am a Muslim so I can quote from my scripture to show how false those who claim Islam is based on evil are. My goal is to love God and love my neighbor. As Prophet Muhammad put it "None of you really has faith until he wishes for his brother what he wishes for himself." To me, that means striving selflessly to make our country and world a better place. This message is no different from another messenger of God, Jesus, in various quotations attributed to him.

It is a very powerful lesson because it means not responding to the words beckoning to fear of the other, but to rise to love your neighbor, which in this increasingly global village is the rest of humanity. The message from the extremists is also very clear; fear your neighbors and, if possible, hate them and maybe even do harm to them. This has not changed whether it is referring to the 1930s and 40s in Europe or to the present day.

Extremists on all sides, Muslims included, say the same thing, proving the angel's worst fears, as related in the Qur'an, when they discussed with God the creation of mankind, who would have freedom to do good and bad. **"Would you place on earth one who would create mischief and shed blood?"** the angels asked, and God replied to the Angels: **"I know what you know not."**

This suggests that God trusted us to do better, to be better! For we have in God's breath divinely guided wisdom and higher

227

intellect with an ethical dimension, unique to humanity. These are the tools required to be better and rise higher in spirituality.

We must overcome and fight the urge to vilify and hate each other. So I challenge you, don't believe the stories you may hear of Muslim bogey men and terror cells throughout America. They are not based in reality. Don't believe that 80% of mosques in America are militant as quoted by some extremists. If it was true we would not have just come through a decade and more of freedom from major terror incidents like 9/11 in America.

Don't believe those whose inner insecurity and need for attention can be very compelling. Misery loves company and those who live in fear want others to live in fear because it makes them feel less isolated. Those hate mongers promise doom and gloom but most of us see a much more vibrant and positive future in trusting and loving than in fearing and hating.

But where do we begin? It begins with you, the reader, taking the first step. You have to decide not to be a foot soldier of hate, regurgitating and passing on e-mails of hate or worse. It means overcoming fear with education from the correct sources about who your neighbor is. Remember learn about your neighbor from them, not those who fear or hate them.

Finally, be courageous enough to invite your neighbor to your place of worship or even your home. There are hundreds, no thousands of opportunities to get to know each other through outreach, and often it comes from a lay person asking his neighbor or friend out to a meal. It takes courage to be the first to make peace and that is why Jesus spoke so highly of the peacemaker. It takes courage to overcome our fears and that is why loving thy neighbor is so important. Those who receive love unconditionally learn to give it back and lose the tendency to hate those they don't know.

Remember that Muslims in the U.S. are only 1% of the population but comprise 10% of our nation's physicians and we are generally well integrated in this society. I became a physician and a cardiologist to heal, and in that job never to ask what race or religion my patients are. For people who don't know me, to accuse me with the broad strokes they accuse Muslims of, just because of my spiritual belief is deeply hurtful.

It isn't easy for a Muslim to walk into a synagogue or a church in America and speak about Islam, nor to write this book, God knows I am not a natural writer. But once we did, we felt free and an integral part of the healing process. I assure you, the vast majority of practicing Muslims want to live in peace and American Muslims want to make this, our nation, a better place. We are an educated nation and we have to be able to overcome our fears through education.

I have a lot of faith in our youth, a generation that looks at us and says "Can't we just get along?" I have heard that, not just from the Muslims, but from young people of all faith communities. They have a worldview that seems less tainted, less prejudiced and more forgiving than their elders. They have understood the concept of a global village that has nothing to do with a global battlefield. They seem to understand "love thy neighbor" better than previous generations have done. Our duty is to preserve and encourage their youthful optimism and never influence it negatively through our fears.

I am optimistic about the future. I welcome you to join me in this optimism. Let's follow Rev. Martin Luther King Jr. and dream of a better tomorrow. God gives us challenges but we have been given guides, in the form of messengers, to help us discern truth from falsehood. Their message calls to a higher level of dialogue, of tolerance, and of understanding and loving each other. It is not just in the *Bible* and the *Torah*, it is very much in the *Qur'an* too.

The American Muslim community has come through a tough period, and we are stronger for it. Through this experience, we have a new and profound respect for this country and its laws. It is these founding laws that have, and will protect us from those who want to hurt us through anti Muslim acts, including anti-*Shariah* legislation, legislation meant to deepen fear and distrust and not meant to address reality. People have been misled in some instances to vote for this legislation in the most un-American, unpatriotic and divisive of ways.

We trust the Constitution of this nation, as it has already deemed these laws illegal in many states and hopefully will deem this hate legislation illegal throughout this nation. It is as though our founding fathers knew that there would be bigots who would come along wanting to vilify one group or another and they encompassed this in this nation's supreme law.

It is a very slippery slope to insist on one's own rights while insulting and hurting the other, pretending this was a part of our Constitution or Bill of Rights. Yes we are given the right of free speech, but it was meant to be the right to petition government when we see things going wrong, not to find ever more hurtful ways of insulting each other.

The American Muslim community, as the newest group of immigrants, is a vibrant and entrepreneurial one. We are younger and better educated than the average Muslim throughout the world. We are the most diverse faith community in America. These are strengths that will ensure we don't blindly follow extremists.

The biggest challenge we all have, as citizens of this nation, is overcoming our fears and staying united. As American Muslims, our vision is making our chosen country the better for our presence, because we value its laws. Not long ago we were a nation beckoning to others through our moral compass. Now, we have lost some ground, but our challenge is gaining that back and we should not back away from that goal. We must continue welcoming immigrants, often the backbone of our workforce to our shores, because that is how we have become the vibrant country that we are.

Our Founding Fathers crafted the Constitution understanding the fact that most of the people who came to the United States came and would come to escape persecution in their homelands, because of ethnic and religious tension. It is ironic then, that although most of the original immigrants came from Europe to escape the religious intolerance there, those who spread fear look to Europe for direction in intolerance. Thankfully, our nation has all the means to protect against that bigotry and, I believe, the vast majority of people in this nation will not give in to this hateful rhetoric.

History will judge us on whether we were able to overcome our prejudices and fears and build a better tomorrow together.

To be able to bring us together in times of fear, and make us reflect, is the quality of great visionaries. I submit to you that great leaders like the great divinely guided messengers from Moses to Jesus to Muhammad, had a profound effect on the people for this reason, and that is why their legacy lives on. But they aren't the only ones who left a great legacy.

Mahatma Gandhi advocated for non-violence and reflection against a brutal colonial occupier, Martin Luther King advocated peaceful persistence in African American civil rights struggles, and Nelson Mandela spent a large part of his life in jail to build a better society.

Their legacy is that they made us reflect and created a huge impact on society through that. Yes, we need a person who can bring us that clarity of vision when we are being torn apart by difficulty and strife. That person can be you, no, must be you. Understand that those great leaders did not come to a perfect world. They were able to do what they did because their homelands needed to move in a different direction.

We have the first ingredient in that we have a very broken world at the moment and I pray for this type of human reflection that cultivates sages. There is nothing to prevent the next sage from being "Made in America".

I believe in the power of prayer and so, in conclusion, I pray for the future. I pray that this nation will emerge stronger and more open minded because of all we have gone through in this last decade and more. Our country is not known for lame excuses and blaming others. I pray that it will emerge stronger and be that beacon of light that the Statue of Liberty still represents, for written on it is:

"Give me your tired, your poor, give me your huddled masses yearning to breathe free, the wretched refuse of your teeming shore. Send these, the tempest-tost to me, I lift my lamp beside the golden door."

That, more than anything, should shine a light on where we should go from here in opening that golden door and welcoming this freedom seeking person described. This book beckons to that welcome and the embracing spirit beyond the golden door, which is difficult at times, but it must be done for our nation to survive and our people to move to better and brighter futures. It is what our founders imagined and bestowed to us to preserve. Let us not let them down nor let our children down. I pray that our children inherit a country morally, ethically and spiritually superior to the nation we were born in, where respect for one another at home and abroad shows the rest of the world a light to be guided by. Aameen/Amen!

APPENDIX – ISLAM EXPLAINED

Chapter 1

Belief in Islam

An 'Open House' is an opportunity to get to know your neighbor by meeting them and sharing a meal with them. Although you may never have met a Muslim, I want to humanize that experience for you so that it will be the first step in meeting your neighbor and feeling less afraid of him/her. I will explain who we are and what our faith really is, as best as I can. I want you to read about my faith from me, not those who fear me.

Religion in Islam is an intensely personal and unique relationship between you and your creator and sustainer. It is the spirituality that people explain as a connection with the divine. Some people seek this spirituality without religion and, although to some this may make sense, to people of faith, and I write as a

Muslim, it seems to bypass the very step required to get to that spiritual station we yearn for. To make an analogy, it is like going from point A to point B without a mode of transport. To understand that spirituality, there are passages of the Qur'an addressing the individual in the most personal and intimate way possible. To quote one such verse God says:

"Tell my devotees who ask you concerning Me, I am indeed close to them, I listen to the prayer of every supplicant when he/she calls on me, so let them also listen to My call and believe in Me that they may walk on the right path" Qur'an 2:186.

This is one of my favorite verses because it appeals to humanity not to give up, that God is intimately aware of our individual situations. It calls us to come back to God – a kind of motherly embrace in a time of intense need.

This is a verse that has helped me more than once in my darkest hours of self doubt and dejection. To know that God is with me and that He hears me and that He knows my situation intimately and also that He is in complete control, gave me a huge amount of solace, when I felt I was not in control. At a higher level of understanding it appeals to mankind to seek and find truth, and ultimately direction in life, through belief and faith. The knowledge that God is intimately aware of our situation helps us not to get so affected by our life situation which could otherwise destroy us.

Islam literally means submission to the will of God and comes from the root word 'Salaam', which means peace. Muslims understand Islam to mean submission to the will of God so that we can attain inner peace and serenity within ourselves, and peace within our societies.

So what does it mean to submit to the will of God? It means that we accept what life situation we are placed in, in a positive and embracing way, without pining for what we do not have. It does not mean resigning ourselves to our 'fate' without struggling to make things better for ourselves and society. This 'struggle' is literally the best definition of Jihad and is the best translation of the word 'Jihad' in the Qur'an. Jihad is best defined as the struggle to live life with the highest standards ethically and morally and to be the best person you can be, through consciousness of God. The prophet, explaining how you submit to your life situation advised:

> *"Look at the less fortunate among you and then you will understand how much you have, instead of looking at those who have more than you and bemoaning what you do not have."*

Muslims get guidance from two sources; the Qur'an, which we believe is literally God's revealed word to Muhammad (the final messenger of God), and the Sunnah, the teachings and example of this last messenger, Muhammad (God's peace be upon him).

Without going into too much detail, the Qur'an was revealed over a period of 23 years. Revelation began with the simple word "Read/recite!" The prophet protested, "I cannot read!", as he was unlettered or illiterate in that he could not read or write. The voice of Arch-angel Gabriel repeated "Recite" and squeezed the prophet after which he repeated the words that were revealed to him through the arch-angel. This is the beginning of revelation and is the beginning of Chapter 96 of the Qur'an and foretold in the Old Testament in Isaiah 29: 11-12 almost verbatim.

The belief system in Islam has six components. The first and most important principle of belief is to believe in One God. We use the term 'Allah' as it is the Arabic term that means 'The One God". Allah cannot be gendered or pluralized as we do not get into the debate of whether God is male or female – God is above the concept of gender. That is why Muslims prefer to use that word, as do Christians, in their Arabic translations of The Bible. We believe that Allah is the same monotheistic God worshipped by Jews and Christians. The Hebrew word, Elohim (royal plural), and the Aramaic word, Allaha, mean exactly the same as Allah. You can see the similarity in addressing the divine in all three Semitic languages.

The second principle of belief is in angels. Starting with Arch-Angel Gabriel, who brought revelation and guidance to all the great messengers, from Abraham to Moses to Jesus to Muhammad – peace be upon them all, and extending to our individual guardian angels. Muslims believe that angels are made out of light and are a creation generally not seen by human beings as they are in a different dimension. They are in a constant state of worship and obedience to God, as they do not have the free will to choose good from evil. There are many thousands of angels and they have specific responsibilities including guardians of the heavens, of punishment and angels that watch over the earth and of humanity.

Contrary to Judeo-Christian theology, Satan is not regarded as an angel, as angels do not have the ability to oppose God's will. Satan, instead, is regarded as part of a different creation called Jinn. Jinn are created of smokeless fire and have the ability to choose between good and evil, similar to human beings. Satan was one of the best of his creation at one time and therefore was raised in rank to the exalted assembly of angels but was still of the Jinn creation. Being Jinn, he had the ability to oppose God's decision to ennoble human kind and thus to be destined for destruction through his/her arrogance, as he refused to obey or submit to God's will.

The third principle of belief is in the divinely revealed books that were sent to guide humanity. In the story of the creation of mankind, when Adam and Eve were expelled from the garden, they asked God for forgiveness. In Islam God forgives them and therefore there is no 'Original Sin' in Islam. What is more, God does not abandon us on earth but promises to guide us, which he has done through divine revelation and divinely guided messengers. These books of guidance include the scriptures that were sent to Abraham, the Psalms to David, the Torah to Moses, the Gospel to Jesus as well as the Qur'an, the final revelation, to Muhammad - peace be upon all these great messengers. The Islamic belief from the Qur'an is that Muhammad, the last messenger, was sent after a break in messengers, to clarify the message. Therefore, Islam is not considered by Muslims as a new religion that started with Prophet Muhammad but merely a continuation and clarification of the oft repeated message of guidance to humanity through belief in God and living a life dedicated to good deeds.

The fourth principle is the belief in all the divinely guided messengers, including the above mentioned messengers, but also more than 100,000 prophets bringing guidance to all of mankind. The stories of some of these prophets are mentioned in the Qur'an and include some of the Hebrew prophets but also many others that are not part of the Old Testament. The Islamic understanding is that God sent guides to all of humanity at various times and renewed that message through other prophets so that man is in a constant state of guidance if they choose to follow the guides that are sent.

These guides stopped with the final messenger Muhammad, only because his miracle was a book that would be preserved in its original form till the day of account, as is promised in the Qur'an by God. That book, revealed in Arabic, is preserved since the time of the prophet, in its original Arabic form, as the Qur'an. It has of course been translated into many languages, but we understand that in translation you do lose part of the message and therefore we turn to the Arabic form to understand the true message.

The fifth principle is the belief in 'The Day of Account' when souls will be sorted out in ranks according to their spiritual closeness to God. Although there is an accounting process that takes place, we understand that most of us will fall short in terms of our good deeds and, ultimately, will look to God's mercy to enter His heavenly bliss. It is to reassure us about this day that Prophet Muhammad narrates that God has reserved ninety nine parts out of a hundred parts of His mercy. All the mercy you see on earth, including the mercy and love that a mother has for her offspring, comes from that one part out of a hundred that remains. That is why barring one chapter, every chapter of the Qur'an begins "In the Name of God, the Most forgiving and Compassionate, the Most Merciful"

The sixth principle is the belief that God gave us the power to choose between good and evil, understanding that they were both created by God and that God knows all that happens and is in ultimate control of everything. This is sometimes referred to as predestination but it is a concept much more complex than predestination, as that gives the impression that man is just a passive vessel of God's plan. That is clearly not the case; it is a dynamic relationship that we have complete freedom over. To put it very simply it means that God is in ultimate control over the major events, including our birth and death, but we have the freedom to choose how we live within those limits. Although human beings are constrained by time, God is above the concept of time and therefore knows all of what will happen.

When you review the principles of belief you can see how close we all are in belief and in the next chapter you will see the similarities of worship as well. You can now see how warped a mind must be to hope for the destruction of the other. No, we are in this together – only hoping to please God through what we do. I wish for all of us the best and the best ending.

Chapter 2

Worship Practices in Islam

The five pillars of faith are the active worship components of
faith, which begins with the central one – the '*shahada*', which is an
active bearing witness that there is none worthy of worship but the
One God, and that Muhammad is a messenger of God, with no
deific quality. Prophet Muhammad is no different from all other
messengers in being a human messenger of a divine message. In
fact, when the prophet had a letter sent to the Christian King of
Abyssinia he is reported to have begun "I bear witness that there is
none worthy of worship but the One God and Jesus and
Muhammad are messengers of God".

This '*shahada*' is the most important pillar as it means an
active *BEARING WITNESS* (which means the highest level of
certainty) through learning about the faith and one's life experience
that there is only One God and the message brought through
Prophet Muhammad is the true message. The '*shahada*' is what is

said when accepting Islam as one's faith and should be felt sincerely from the heart and said with the tongue. This is why when one accepts Islam as one's religion and way of life he/she is always asked whether this decision was made under any duress, as faith should never be forced. An active bearing witness – is the highest level of certainty, even in a court of law. **"There is no compulsion in religion"**, the Qur'an proclaims, **"because truth is clear from error"**.

The second pillar of faith is prayer five times a day, something that I have grown to love more and more as it is a spiritual break that I have for myself during a busy day at work. That one on one time with my Creator and Sustainer that makes Him, The Almighty, so accessible to each of us at all times of the day. It is a discourse and reassurance from our creator, and a reminder at several times during the day that the purpose of life is to attain closeness to God and this life must be one that is constantly put in its true perspective.

Prayer is such an important pillar that Prophet Muhammad was summoned from Makkah to Jerusalem, to the site of Al-Aqsa, where he prayed with all the other prophets of the past. He was then taken, accompanied by Angel Gabriel, to an audience with God where he was commanded to pray five times a day. It is so important a pillar that even if we are sick and cannot get up we are supposed to pray lying down, to constantly remember God in sickness and health.

The third pillar of faith is giving a fixed percentage of our wealth to the poor and needy, called 'zakat' or the poor due, and is regarded as a purification of one's wealth. The literal translation of the Arabic word 'zakat' means purification. We calculate this amount annually and give 2.5% of our wealth in zakat. There are specific categories of people that we give to, such as the poor, the homeless, the orphan, the traveler and several other categories of people. If not given, it is considered an unpaid debt to the poor that we will be held accountable for. Imam Ali, the fourth Caliph of Islam, reminisced that had people taken zakat seriously and given it correctly, there would be no starvation on earth.

The fourth pillar of faith is fasting in the month of Ramadan. Ramadan is the ninth month of the Islamic lunar calendar. We do not eat, drink or have marital relations from dawn to sunset daily for the month. It is regarded as a way of building God consciousness and is done in gratitude to God for revelation sent to mankind throughout time. Muslims believe that all revelation came down during this lunar month of Ramadan. So we fast in gratitude for guidance sent to Jews and Christians and all other people of guidance, as we fast in gratitude for our own guidance. Fasting however is not considered to be merely staying hungry and thirsty, but it is a time of contemplation, reflection and improving yourself. As the prophet said "God is not in need of your staying away from food and drink, if you cannot stay away from evil speech and evil deeds."

The final pillar is the pilgrimage to Makkah, the place where Abraham and Ishmael built/rebuilt the first house for the worship of God, thought to be on the site of the house built originally by Adam, the first human being on earth. The pilgrimage is truly an enlightening experience. Each male pilgrim dresses in two pieces of white unstitched cloth, showing our absolute equality in front of God. Women are allowed to wear more clothing for issues of modesty. This equality is regarded as a reminder of the Day of Account when we will be presented to God without any difference between us, except the difference in closeness to God through our good actions.

During the pilgrimage, we remember the miraculous saving of Ishmael's life as a baby in the desert. Hagar, Ishmael's mother, was left with the baby Ishmael in the desert and when they ran out of food and water she ran up and down two hills looking for anybody who could help, a ritual followed by pilgrims to this day. Finally, the baby Ishmael's thirst was quenched by Angel Gabriel who caused a spring to gush out of the ground, which to this day serves all the pilgrims that visit the desert town, Makkah, in present day Saudi Arabia. When we run between these two hills we actively remember that we are running in the footsteps of a woman, the leader of this part of the Hajj ritual, honoring her and women in general, especially for the sacrifices they go through for their children.

We also remember Ishmael's adulthood during the pilgrimage when he joined his father, Abraham, to build the house of worship to God. It is after the building of the house that Abraham is told by

Angel Gabriel to make the call to prayer and when he questions the need for a call, saying it was just him and his family, Angel Gabriel reminds Abraham that his duty is only to do the calling and the results are entirely in the hands of God. It is in response to this call that every pilgrim calls out "Here we are O Our Lord, here we are" in response to that original call of Abraham.

We contemplate Abraham's willingness to sacrifice his son at the command of God, and his ultimate sacrifice of a ram instead of his son (at the command of God, through Arch-Angel Gabriel) in a supreme act of faith, that is related through all the three major monotheistic faiths Judaism, Christianity and Islam.

This gives you a rough idea of the belief system and practices of Islam. It is not a new religion as Islam, which literally means submission to the will of God, began with the first human beings Adam and Eve. In our commonalities it gives us a level of kinship, in particular with the Jews and Christians, known as the 'people of the book', that received divine revelation before us, and have a very similar belief system. It makes us, as those who have been given revelation, more responsible as we have been "chosen" to be given revelation so that we may show an example to others by this revelation on how to live life purposefully. How far short we all fall in this responsibility. It is not a privilege that we are given but a responsibility, and the privilege we achieve is only through fulfilling that responsibility. So how are we, "the guided ones", so misguided in going to wars and killing so mercilessly, while each of us claims to be the follower of the Most Merciful? Life is a challenge for each of us and our goal must be in our small way to change this paradigm.

Chapter 3

Jihad, Shariah, and Other Misconceptions

Apart from the belief system and ritual practices that I have explained, the spirituality of Islam can be appreciated in the details of the practices, where the daily prayers are a direct conversation with our Creator. When we begin our prayer with praising and glorifying God, He announces to the exalted assembly of angels "My servant ... is calling on me." And the conversation proceeds from there. That is why it is natural for you to see Muslims cry in prayer while beseeching God during supplication. There is no intermediary needed when praying, confessing or supplicating to God in Islam.

Through contemplating this spiritual connection to God in Islam, there was an era in which some of the greatest poets and scholars thrived. Rumi, one such poet, writes eloquently about the love of God in some of the most beautiful poetry and is one of the most popular poets in the West, including the United States. This does not come in isolation from himself but it comes from the beautiful tradition of the Prophet, who speaks about 'Ihsan', which means perfection of faith about which he said "pray as though you see God for even though you don't, know that God sees you". These are the concepts that later scholars illustrated through poetry, as Rumi did. So also did the whole Sufi movement that yearned for spirituality through religion, which is different from the spirituality that people now yearn for without committing to religion. This is difficult for Muslims to understand as spirituality must be rooted in the love of God for a Muslim.

Religion becomes closed spiritually to one who comes with a closed mind, full of arrogance, in a quest to find fault as opposed to the person who is humbly seeking guidance. For those throughout time who have come seeking guidance the Qur'an has opened many avenues for inner peace, serenity and true contentment and that is the reason Islam is the fastest growing religion in America and in the world. It is not something to fear but something to investigate and understand and benefit from.

People do not throng to a religion that preaches hate and violence. That is so alien to true Islam. For some, however, there is always a need to use small differences to perpetuate hate and that is true of the Protestant-Catholic divide in Northern Ireland, as it is the Sunni-Shia divide in Iraq where we have seen so much violence.

What we hope is that the majority of our neighbors, when they get to know who we are, will realize that we are also in this quest to find inner peace and spiritual contentment. We must learn to do this respecting our differences. That comes with maturity and self confidence in faith, and is hindered by self doubt and fear of the other.

It is important for me, in this book, to address certain misconceptions about Islam with regard to Arabic and Islamic terms and practices. These concepts have been used to spread so much fear that they need to be clarified.

One of those terms is '*Jihad*'. *Jihad* literally means struggle, and is understood to be the inner struggle to live life to the highest moral and ethical standards you can. This is also the most common reference to *Jihad* in the Qur'an. It is a struggle because it means a lifelong quest to be the best that you can. That could be in your work to ease people's suffering as a physician, or as a mother bringing up her child to the best of her ability, sacrificing other pleasures to do that and doing it with the higher purpose of serving God and humanity.

Muslims understand *Jihad* to have two levels of understanding: an individual struggle to be the best human being you can, and a societal struggle to be an ideal society, caring for the least of us and standing up against the oppression of anyone in society.

This second societal responsibility is to try to develop a just society which entails standing up against oppression and tyranny and striving to establish a society with social equity and justice. This means making sure that you take care of the poor and homeless, as a societal responsibility, to make the world a better place. As has been said "the measure of a civilization is how it treats its weakest members". This is similar in concept to 'Tikun Olam' in Judiasm – "healing the world".

Sometimes this societal responsibility means standing up against oppression to achieve justice. Fighting may be required to achieve this goal. *Jihad* is not a random declaration to fight, but needs to come from a central authority of scholars, weighing the pros and cons, before a decision to go to war.

An example of a war seeking justice and to prevent oppression is the Bosnian war, when NATO forces defended the Bosnians from genocide at the hands of the Serbs. If there is gross injustice, in similar circumstances, under the proper authority, *Jihad* can be declared and would entail fighting in defense of the oppressed. These oppressed do not have to be Muslims, as justice should be practiced on principle, regardless of the relationship or situation of the perpetrator of injustice.

Now, knowing the true concept of *Jihad*, you understand why it was very problematic when one refers to terrorists as *Jihadists*. That makes it seem like the terrorists are fighting a just war against oppression and tyranny, which is far from the case. That is certainly not what we want the terrorists to feel they are doing, although they would love to be given that honor, nor do we want our youth to feel that the terrorists are fighting a just war against oppression, which we worry may explain why some Muslim youth are going over to fight there. It also gives the impression that the 'War on Terror' is a war against Islam, because *Jihad* is a legitimate concept in Islam.

It sent shivers down our spines when politicians like Donald Rumsfeld and Dick Cheney, and now Ted Cruz and Donald Trump, use *Jihadist* in place of terrorist, as this 'legitimizes' their barbaric terrorism. As a result, Muslims welcomed the change in tone when the Obama administration took office and called terrorists by their proper term and differentiating religious terms from the 'War on Terror'.

Another common term that is misunderstood, and deliberately misconstrued by some, is the term '*shariah*'. '*Shariah*' literally means 'the path' and in Islam is used to mean the path to God or the path to salvation or success. *Shariah* guidelines come from our two sources of guidance, the *Qur'an* – God's revealed message and the *Sunnah* – the prophetic example and his teachings. These include guidelines on prayer, fasting, giving in charity and living a life in as ethical and moral a way as possible. *Shariah* also includes guidelines concerning marriage and divorce and how we take care of the dying and how we bury the dead. It is instructive on caring for the poor and being fair and just to all. It is very similar to Jewish or *Halakhic* laws, which literally means 'to walk' or 'the path'. Muslims understand the similarities to be so because they come, ultimately, from the same source.

Similar to Judaism, Islam, is a way of life and, therefore, came with a code of laws that guided to proper behavior, but it is only a distortion of the punitive part that is ever described by those who spread fear about "*Shariah* law". The media in its discussion of *Shariah*, will often show a vigilante stoning of a woman in

Afghanistan, giving viewers the subtle impression and subliminal message that this is *Shariah*. It would be similar to showing the lynching of African Americans while discussing American law. Everyone should understand that those are both examples of vigilante 'street justice' and have nothing to do with either Islamic law or American law and we need to all be more responsible in reporting.

Shariah only gives the broad outlines of how to live in a just society. Using these guidelines scholars of Islam formulate the laws relevant to the time and place they are in. It is a dynamic system of jurisprudence that takes into consideration the guidelines (from the *Qur'an* and *Sunnah* – example of the prophet) and the situation we are in, to come up with a set of laws that temporally and geographically are meant to be adaptable, depending on the circumstance you live in.

Fearmongers often quote stoning as part of "*Shariah* Law". Ironically, stoning is not even mentioned once in the Qur'an. On the other hand, The Bible does call for stoning to death for certain crimes.

Shariah guidelines have guided law in vast parts of the world for centuries, and resulted in some of the most advanced countries, such as Islamic Spain, Al-Andalusia. Certainly, a quarter of the world would not be following this religion, if *Shariah* guidelines were as barbaric as the fear-mongers claim.

Scholars looked at *Shariah* guidelines and came up with six principles that summarized *Shariah*. They are: the right to protection of life, the right to protect your family, the right of education for all, the rights of religious freedom and the right to protect ones property and honor. None of these clash with, and most of these principles are in fact incorporated into, the US laws, through the Constitution and the Bill of Rights. Review them again to really see the similarities to the latter. That is why Muslims aren't going around demanding "*Shariah* in America".

To say "No *Shariah* in America" is a statement of pure ignorance. Ultimately, that is what it boils down to, a lack of knowledge about Islam. In this world of trumped up fear, those who protest against *Shariah* put the cart before the horse and oppose *Shariah*, even if nobody is asking for it.

When it comes to issues of religion, there are many people throughout the world who will use, and have used, religion to cause enormous evil, death, and destruction. It is not the religion but the mindset of those bent on evil that cause this amount of anger and hate in the name of religion. I think a far better way to assess how one should act should be to constantly ask the question "Would my religious role model command or partake in this – whatever the activity you are calling to?" Whether that role model is Moses, Jesus, Muhammad or Gautama Buddha, I am certain that question would guide you to deal with humility, dignity and respect towards the other. This is why in Islam the *Sunnah*, or example of the prophet, is one of our important sources of guidance.

Religion should always be a force for good. Through the Park 51 issue, and Islamophobia in general, the truly religious people said "Not in the name of my religion". For Christians, Rev. David Good, the senior minister of the Congregational Church in Old Lyme, said it best in his Op-Ed where he calls Islamophobia a disease:

> "It is a disease that would shake the very foundations of our country's cherished tradition of liberty and justice for all, make a mockery of our Statue of Liberty and all that it represents, and undermine our country's freedom of religion. And when Islamophobia is spread by those who purport to be Christian, it brings dishonor on the name of Christianity."

This is the true Christian standard, as it holds our actions to the standard of the role model, Jesus, who Muslims and Christians alike revere. In Islam, Jesus is a messenger of God and his life is supposed to be an example to be followed. That is why his life is prominently illustrated in the Qur'an. It is important for Christians and Muslims to be always asking the question "What would Jesus do?", and Muslims know the answer is almost always the same as what Prophet Muhammad would do.

Our relationship with the majority community of this country is of great importance, and our similarities and differences must be understood. The belief system of Islam gives Jesus a revered position as a messenger to whom revelation was sent from God to humanity in the form of The Gospel. We revere Jesus as 'The Messiah', born of a miraculous virgin birth to a revered mother, Mary. We acknowledge Jesus' ability to perform innumerable miracles, including raising from the dead, all done through the will of God. However, Muslims do not accept any divinity to the person of Jesus, nor do the Jews expect 'The Messiah' to be a divine figure. We believe that procreation is a necessary part of propagation for the created and not the Creator.

"And in their footsteps (referring to the Hebrew prophets) we sent Jesus the son of Mary, confirming the law (of the Torah) that had come before him: we sent him the gospel, in it was guidance and light and confirmation of the law that had come before him, a guidance and an admonition to those who are God conscious" (Qur'an 5:46).

This is the translation of a verse of the Holy Qur'an. The Holy Qur'an in Arabic is regarded by Muslims as God's word that was sent through arch-angel Gabriel to Prophet Muhammad, as we believe the original Aramaic Gospel was God's word to Jesus. They were both messengers bringing direct revelation and guidance to humanity.

The head-scarf is another issue that has generated controversy. It has been portrayed as a tool of oppression in some circles especially after France banned it from being worn in public spaces. It is associated with putting down women by those who don't know enough about Islam and, if it is forced, I agree it is wrong. But in the west those who wear the headscarf have made a conscious decision to wear it.

In France, they have embraced the myth of women being forced to wear the headscarf and have equated progress with giving up what these women view as a symbol of their religion and their modesty. It must be viewed as, for example, the orange habit of a Buddhist monk, or the habit that Catholic nuns used to wear, as a sign of religious modesty. To ban it is to interfere with religious freedom and that is clearly a problem for France, especially as it has a very large Muslim minority. It is unnecessarily alienating a minority and setting up division without foresight or wisdom.

Muslim women view the head-scarf as a sign of faith and modesty, and a civilized and mature people should be able to respect diversity and difference. Modesty is an important aspect of Islam and to equate that with being backward is immature and insulting to women who have chosen to wear a head-scarf and to Muslims in general. In fact, Muslim women look to the example of Mary, the mother of Jesus, who is always portrayed as covered from head to toe with only her face, hands and feet exposed.

Muslim women that I have spoken to feel that the headscarf is part of their civil rights struggle. They view it as a form of Islamic feminism, preventing the objectification of their bodies when used for marketing on bill boards. They feel the headscarf is a statement "I am more than an object to be used for marketing, I have a mind and a spiritual soul that I am nurturing through Islam, and the head scarf is a symbol of that." As such, I have enormous respect for these women as they are standing up for their rights against being disrespected and stereotyped, despite the taunts of many.

If some people are saying something negative about a religion that has existed harmoniously, for the most part, for almost 1500 years, bringing huge advances to humanity, and you are being told this religion is the cause of so many problems, think about the sender of such a message. Are they really knowledgeable about this or are they just transmitting and perpetuating somebody else's hateful agenda? Most importantly, ask Muslim friends you know whether the facts you are hearing are true.

I like to quote a friend of mine, the President of Hartford Seminary, who said to me about how she taught her course on 'Dialogue in a World of Difference'. "One must learn about the other through the perspective of the practitioner, not somebody else's perspective of them". This would solve a lot of the fear, spread by hate groups, and allow all of us to really get to know each other better.

Chapter 4

Muhammad, the Messenger of God

The personality of Muhammad, the final messenger of God according to Muslims, has been attacked by some people in their zeal to attack Islam and Muslims. They attack his personal life and distort his public life to make him look like a tyrant, when Muslims know this is far from the truth. They attack his personal life based on the age of his wife at marriage and the number of wives he had, but we cannot use cultural differences which were the norm at that time to paint a different cultural tradition as being 'wrong'.

Many of the prophets of the Hebrew bible had many wives and there are many cultures in which people marry young. A cultural practice at a different time, almost 1500 years ago, which you may disagree with, does not make it wrong. One should not be so arrogant as to define differences in culture as being wrong or inferior.

Muslims in America marry only one wife and the majority of Muslims throughout the Muslim world marry only one wife and this is completely in keeping with Islamic norms. It was a cultural practice at that time that Islam allowed and that is another beauty of Islam. It allowed for unique cultural traditions when those traditions do not directly contradict the faith. This speaks to the embrace of diversity in Islam and accounts for its spread to every continent. If you walk into any mosque in the US you will see how diverse a faith community we really are. It is filled with people of different colors and different accents. Our diversity is a blessing from God and a source of strength. A Pew research poll found us to be the most diverse faith community in America.

In his public life Prophet Muhammad is portrayed as a war-monger when Muslims understand him to be far from that. He preached a message of peaceful coexistence for the first thirteen years of his prophethood; from the age of forty, when he received revelation, until he was fifty three. He was then forced to leave his home in Makkah and migrate to Medina, due to the constant attacks on him and his followers. Despite these repeated attacks, he asked his followers to be patient and to trust in God. It is only after they suffered murders and boycotts, the latter of which led to his wife's death, and their forced expulsion to another land, that revelation was even sent regarding defending the new religion through fighting.

During the final conquest of Makkah, however, when the prophet walked into Makkah at the head of an army of over 10,000 soldiers, victorious over those who had for so long oppressed, attacked, expelled him from his city and then waged war against him repeatedly, his first act was to announce a general amnesty and forgiveness. Even those who were in the house of the Makkan leader, Abu Sufyan, who directed the fight against the prophet for so long, were forgiven and given amnesty.

"This day no reproach shall be on you. God will forgive you; He is the Most Merciful of the Merciful. You can go free!"

It is unimaginable how the faith he preached could be distorted to cause the destruction of 9/11, as terrorists and Islamophobes alike contend. You will find throughout this book that the message of the terrorists and Islamophobes is very similar. They both believe that the terrorists are practicing real Islam in their zeal to misportray/blame Islam. Killing innocent civilians is one of the greatest crimes in Islam and the terrorists will be held accountable for their deeds. Killing in the name of God would require a much more stringent judgment, and God is the Supreme and Just Judge.

I believe those who carried out the terrorist attacks of 9/11 were completely misguided in their understanding of religion. It does not in any way represent the religion Islam or the teachings of God's last messenger, Muhammad. If every believer in religion would stand up against every form of hatred and bigotry, the world would be a better place.

The cartoons of the prophet and the video by a Coptic Christian in California about the prophet, and the response on the Muslim streets, through riots, have highlighted a problem that must be dealt with.

So how did Prophet Muhammad become such a lightning rod for insults and protests? Did it start recently or has this been a constant since the beginning of his delivery of the message? Insults and even physical abuse are not new and, as Muslims, we have to look at the way the prophet responded to those who did this to him. Did he turn the other cheek as Jesus did?

There are many accounts of insults that the prophet endured during the Makkan and Medinan period. The prophet's life and example is very well preserved, in the most well documented way, in the hadith literature. Authentic sayings and teachings are preserved in the most scientific form, through an authentic chain of narrators, for each of the prophet's sayings. This can be traced directly to a companion of the prophet himself.

In the early period of delivering his message in Makkah, Prophet Muhammad was walking along the road when he saw an old woman who was carrying her luggage on her head in the noon day heat. The prophet, on seeing this, came to her aid and asked her whether he could help her.

She acquiesced and throughout the journey she related all the false rumors about the prophet and told him that that was why she was leaving the city. The prophet bore this without a word of protest.

After he had taken her bags to the destination, after thanking him she said to him "I have not even asked you your name?" He replied to her "I am that same Muhammad you are leaving this city because of". His deeds spoke louder than any verbal protest against the accusations she made could ever do.

She was so impressed by the fact that despite all the accusations about him, that he had still helped her without a word of protest, that she said: "If you are that Muhammad, then they misled me into leaving the city. Please take my bags back that I may be guided by you."

Likewise, early on in his prophethood, he was made very uncomfortable in his own city Makkah. Therefore, he decided to leave Makkah and looked for another place to deliver his message from. He went to Taif, a city close to Makkah, but not only did they not listen to him there they sent their kids out to throw stones at him. When he retreated to a garden outside the city and was resting, all bloodied and bruised, an angel of God came down to him and said:

"I have been commanded to follow your order, if you want I will bring down the two mountains on either side of Taif and destroy the people in it (as were destroyed the people of Noah and Lot, for their disobedience and violence towards their prophet)."

To this the prophet replied

"I have not been sent to curse, I was instead sent to guide. If they do not believe perhaps their future generations will believe."

That was his attitude and that is why we revere this man. Even in the height of insult and abuse, he refrained from being reactionary. He never expected us to be reactionary either. He expected us to follow his example and as the Qur'an commands "be patient and constant". That is the example we should try to follow and it is not easy. In his personal life he always turned the other cheek.

Some say that he was only peaceful when he was in Makkah but when he was in Medina he was a warrior. Indeed he was commanded to defend the community against attack, after he was expelled from Makkah, and he did defend himself and his followers at times, but that did not change his calm demeanor when facing aggression against his person.

Once, when he with his wife Ayesha, a group of people went past him and taunted him by saying "Death to you, O Muhammad!" (In Arabic this sounds very similar to peace be with you, the traditional Muslim greeting). Ayesha, on hearing this taunt, reacted angrily saying "and to you be death and the curse of God be with you."

The prophet gently put his hand on hers, holding her back saying "Beware of cursing and getting angry like this." She replied, "Did you hear what they said?" He replied to her "Did you hear what I said?" implying, don't react to what others say or do, listen to my message and follow my example, be the better person.

Similarly, at another time he said:

"Don't be a people without a mind, saying, "if they treat me badly, I will treat them badly, and if they treat me well, I will treat them well", instead get used to doing good regardless of how you are treated."

That is the example we as Muslims revere.

One of the most powerful examples was how the prophet trained his closest companions. Abu Bakr, the prophet's closest companion and the first Caliph of Islam, was once being accused and insulted falsely by a man. This tirade went on for awhile and the prophet stood by Abu Bakr silently. Finally, when Abu Bakr could not take it any longer, he retorted back, at which point the prophet immediately got up and left. Abu Bakr followed him right away and said in protest to the prophet "That is not fair. When he was insulting me you were smiling and when I tried to defend myself you got upset and walked away." The prophet responded in the calmest way by saying; "When he was insulting you, the angels around you were defending you and I was smiling at their defense of you, but when you got angry and retorted in anger, the angels left, and when the angels leave so does the messenger of God."

This is the example that he wanted from his closest companions. Look at the bigger picture. You are demeaning yourself if you react in anger. This is what made Islam supremely successful in the time of the prophet and his close companions. The companions never killed people and stormed places due to insults, and the prophet never killed the ambassadors sent to him.

However, they were strong in defense of justice and against oppression or when they were attacked.

We love him because he taught us how to respect people of other faiths. Once, a delegation of Catholic monks from St Catherine's monastery in Mount Sinai asked him for a letter of protection. In 628 CE, four years before his death, when he was the undisputed leader in Medina, he had this letter penned to them:

This is a message from Muhammad, the son of Abdullah, as a covenant to those who adopt Christianity, near and far, we are with them. Verily I, the servants, the helpers, and my followers defend them, because Christians are my citizens; and by Allah! I hold out against anything that displeases them. No compulsion is to be on them. Neither are their judges to be removed from their jobs nor their monks from their monasteries. No one is to destroy a house of their religion, to damage it, or to carry anything from it to the Muslims' houses. Should anyone take any of these, he would spoil God's covenant and disobey His Prophet. Verily, they are my allies and have my secure charter against all that they hate. No one is to force them to travel or to oblige them to fight. The Muslims are to fight for them. If a female Christian is married to a Muslim, it is not to take place without her approval. She is not to be prevented from visiting her church to pray. Their churches are to be respected. They are neither to be prevented from repairing them nor the sacredness of their covenants. No one of the nation (Muslims) is to disobey the covenant till the Last Day (end of the world).

This is the man we revere and respect because he showed us how to respect those of other faiths, establishing guidelines on freedom of religion even in the family setting.

I like to end this chapter with a few quotes from non-Muslims to show you what a profound effect Prophet Muhammad had on some great personalities that lived and wrote about him.

George Bernard Shaw said: "I have studied him, the wonderful man and in my opinion, far from being the Antichrist (this was the hate rhetoric at that time) he must be called the savior of humanity". "I have always held the religion of Muhammad in high estimation because of its wonderful vitality. It is the only religion which appears to me to possess that assimilating capacity to the changing phase of existence, which can make itself appeal to every age." *The genuine Islam - 1936.*

Michael Hart likewise wrote about Prophet Muhammad when he ranked him first among the hundred most influential persons in history "My choice of Muhammad to lead the list of the world's most influential persons maybe a surprise to some and maybe questioned by others, but he was the only man in history who was supremely successful on both the religious and secular levels." *The 100: A ranking of the most influential persons in history - 1978*

Lamartine, a French historian wrote "If greatness of purpose, smallness of means, and astounding results are the three criteria of human genius, who could dare to compare any great man in modern history with Muhammad? The most famous men created arms, laws and empires only. They founded, if anything at all no more than material powers which often crumbled away before their eyes. This man not only moved armies, legislation, empires, peoples and dynasties, but millions of men in one third of the then inhabited world; and more than that he moved altars, the gods, the religions, the ideas, the beliefs and souls... Philosopher, orator, apostle, legislator, warrior, conqueror of ideas, restorer of rational dogmas, of a cult without images, the founder of twenty terrestrial empires and one spiritual empire, that is Muhammad. As regards all the standards by which human greatness may be measured, we may well ask, is there any man greater than he?" *Histoire de la Turquie - 1854*

Sarojini Naidu a famous Indian poetess wrote "It was the first religion that preached and practiced democracy; for in the mosque, when the call for prayers is sounded and worshippers are gathered together, the democracy of Islam is embodied five times a day when the peasant and king kneel side by side and proclaim "God alone is great". I have been struck over and over again by this indivisible unity of Islam that makes man instinctively a brother" *Ideals of Islam 1918.*

Mahatma Gandhi wrote "I wanted to know the best of one who holds today's undisputed sway over the hearts of millions of mankind. I became more than convinced that it was not the sword that won a place for Islam in those days in the scheme of life. It was the rigid simplicity, the utter self effacement of the prophet, the scrupulous regard for his pledges, his intense devotion to his friends and followers, his intrepidity, his fearlessness, his absolute trust in God and in his own mission. These and not the sword carried everything before them and surmounted every obstacle. When I closed the second volume (of the prophet's biography), I was sorry there was not more for me to read of the great life." *Young India journal*

This is the man that Muslims revere so much that when he is insulted by those who don't know him, simply to spread hate, there is a sense of hurt among all Muslims and some react through anger, despite his teachings to the contrary. He was, in my opinion, the greatest man to walk the earth and knowing him, through the proper sources available, will only make you a better person.

It is important for Muslims in positions deemed to be respected in America such as physicians, engineers, teachers, social workers, business people and others to speak out and clarify our faith. We have to take back the image of Islam that is being distorted by others and be the true image of Islam.

Muslims in America are some of the most well educated, wealthy (per capita) and entrepreneurial Muslims in world. We are the best people to represent ourselves and we cannot afford to lose this opportunity, nor abdicate our responsibilities to those loud voices, from within and without Islam, that distort who we are. Our neighbors demand we stand up and represent ourselves and not let them remain in fear of us. They deserve nothing less from us!